THE CALL OF SEDONA

THE CALL OF SEDONA

Journey of the Heart

Ilchi Lee

BEST
LIFE

BEST
LIFE

BEST Life Media
6560 State Route 179, Ste. 114
Sedona, AZ 86351
www.bestlifemedia.com
1-877-504-1106

This book should be regarded as a reference source and is not intended to replace professional medical advice. Seek the advice of your physician before beginning this or any other fitness program. The author and the publisher disclaim any liability arising directly or indirectly from the use of this book.

First paperback edition: August 2011
Library of Congress Control Number: 2011932370
ISBN-13: 978-1-935127-48-2

Whatever path brought you here
There is a reason why you came,
Though you may not know it now.

So please open your ears and listen.
Listen to the message that Sedona has for you.
The old juniper standing tall in the golden sunset
    just might reveal it to you.

TABLE OF CONTENTS

ACKNOWLEDGMENTS

I WOULD LIKE TO THANK Michelle Seo, Daniel Graham, and Mina Kim for their interpretation and translation. Their constant support helped me communicate with Western minds. I also wish to thank Peter Hayes for his thoughtful editing. Thanks are also due to Hyerin Moon and Jiyoung Oh for their support and assistance in bringing this book to fruition at BEST Life Media. Special thanks should be given to Franklin Hughes and Hyerin Moon for their beautiful pictures that captured the sacred moments of Sedona.

AUTHOR'S INTRODUCTION

I RARELY STAY IN ONE PLACE for more than a few months. That's because traveling the world and meeting and speaking with people is my life's work. Nonetheless, Sedona is the land I love the most on this earth. Whatever place I'm coming from, when I head back to Sedona and start to see its red rocks in the distance, my heart and breath open up and my mind becomes calm as though I've come home.

Sedona is a flower blooming in the Arizona desert. The land here is a deep red, the sky an endless blue. Between that red earth and blue sky, there flows a sacred atmosphere. Not only are there red rocks, green juniper trees, cacti, and a burning sun, but there are also ravines and steep gorges where clear water flows and wooded forests are soaked with the golden hues of autumn. This arid land that pours out such a primordial power has a unique ability to awaken within us the greatest of spirits.

My First Visit

I first came to Sedona in January 1996. At the time, I was yet another tourist among many, drawn by its beauty and mystery. Now, fifteen years later, I can't imagine my life without Sedona. To me, Sedona is the most comfortable home as well as a most divine and sacred land. It's the friend with whom I feel the closest of connections, the "seuseung," or spiritual guide, who always awakens me anew.

I have received many messages while in Sedona, such as when I sat atop Bell Rock, looking down at the river embraced by red stone; when I walked along the banks of Oak Creek and quietly watched the full moon reflected in its water; and when I stood on Schnebly Hill and was mesmerized by the flames of the sunset in the western sky . . . Sedona has spoken to me.

The messages I received from Sedona were, at first, almost like fantasies, for Sedona always told me to dream dreams that seemed impossible; at times, it even caused in me agonizing dilemmas that were difficult to bear.

But I had to listen to those messages. When the messages of Sedona reverberated in the deepest parts of my heart, even if they seemed "a ridiculous thing to do" from a rational perspective, I just focused on them unconditionally. Whenever I was having a hard time, I would turn to the rocks and trees that had lived so much longer than human beings; I borrowed a lot of strength from the moon and the stars of Sedona that were awake in the dead of night when the world was fast asleep. This is how the things that seemed at first like fantasies became realities, one by one. And many others were drawn to participate in them, too.

Sedona gave me a dream. It gave me constant inspiration and strength so that my dream would not die, no matter the hardships I found myself facing. To me, everything in the US used to be so foreign, including the language and the culture. Through Sedona, I gained the strength to truly settle here. I gained a new inspiration that enabled me to share my enlightenment and training methods with the whole world, and it is here that I met so many friends and supporters. Though I was well past middle age, I also opened myself to a new creativity and artistic capacity that was rising inside of me. This is the place where I developed the Earth Citizen spirit as a philosophy, and where I heard the message of Mago, which means Mother Earth.

In order to repay the blessings I received from Sedona, I worked hard to share with other people what I felt and discovered through Sedona. That's why I love Sedona as much as I love my life. With every step I take upon this red and sacred earth, I am filled with deep gratitude and affection.

Sedona is truly a sacred and blessed land. When I stand on a hill of red rock and look into the distance where heaven and earth meet at the horizon, or when an immense, round moon rises so close that it feels like I could just reach and touch it with my hand, what arises within me is a lucid awareness that I'm living on a star called "Earth," and I find myself deeply and vividly moved. The heart of the earth opens my heart and enters, becoming one with me. And concern for people and the world arises from the deepest part of my being, along with a powerful desire to take care of them. The messages of Sedona, this land graced with beauty and wonder from time immemorial, always make my heart vibrate with strength and love as intense as the very redness of its earth.

This Book

This book contains the stories about the messages that I received from Sedona. It also has stories about my life, which I have lived by following those messages. And this book can also become your story.

The essence of the message that Sedona has conveyed to me is that inside each one of us there is a much greater and more beautiful truth and dream than the ordinary ones we know. And that we already have everything we need to achieve them.

I hope that, through this book, you realize that you have always been great and that you will gain fresh inspiration and a dream that will infuse vitality into your life. Finally, I hope that you can take part in the beautiful dream that Sedona gives through its profound connection with the earth.

What lends meaning and value to our daily life is always our dreams. If you need a dream—or if you need to rediscover a dream you've lost—come here to Sedona.

Ilchi Lee
Sedona, April 2011

1 THE DAWN OF A NEW ENLIGHTENMENT

I N EARLY 1996, I was reading a newspaper in Los Angeles when I saw a photo that immediately grabbed my attention. "Hey, where is this place?" I asked. The red rocks were so real they felt like they might jump out of the paper at me. I read the caption beneath the photo and learned it was a place called Sedona, in the state of Arizona.

I couldn't get there fast enough; I wanted to see those red rocks, so I asked an acquaintance to come with me. It was a long drive of nearly eight hours. We cruised along from Los Angeles to Flagstaff until we came to Sedona. It was the middle of the night, so we settled into a motel that hugged Oak Creek Canyon.

It was a dark night, so there was little chance to see the scenery aside from the sparkling stars that filled the night

sky with their refreshing twinkling. I wondered what Sedona would look like when I opened my eyes in the morning. As I filled my lungs with its clean, crisp air, I went to sleep with excitement and anticipation in my heart.

As soon as I opened my eyes the next morning, I threw back the curtains. The view was of a mountain of blended red and white rocks, standing tall above the verdant juniper trees. At the top of the mountain were large and small rocks shaped like various animals. Then I saw one that caught my attention. At a flat part on the top, there was a modest rock whose form resembled a person meditating while seated in the lotus position.

I thought to myself, "Wow, even the rocks in Sedona meditate!"

I couldn't tell whether that was true or if those were the only rocks my eyes could see, no matter where I looked, but my initial feeling was very good.

After a simple breakfast, I wandered about Sedona, here and there, wherever I felt like going. It seemed like the entire city was embraced by arms of red rock. The green of the junipers and cacti that dotted the red turf proffered a dramatic contrast of color. The sky of Sedona, wrapped around the red burnt earth, seemed clearer and bluer than any sky I'd seen. There was a sanctity circulating in the air between earth and heaven. Though it was winter, warm sunlight was shining down through the clear air. As I looked at the dazzling beauty of Sedona's earth and sky awash with the morning sun, my heart skipped a beat, and it occurred to me that this just might be the place for which I had been searching for so long.

I came to the US from Korea in 1993 to share the traditional Korean mind-body training methods known as Dahnhak (which became Dahn Yoga in the US). At the time, the Dahn Centers that I had established in Korea had increased to around fifty and I was sharing a modernized and systematized form of Dahnhak with many people.

I handed over the management of the Korean Dahn Centers to my students and started anew in the US with a pioneering spirit. The place where I first settled with my students was New Jersey. It was not easy, however, to put our roots down in a land where the culture and even the language were so unfamiliar. Our first attempts were ones of trial and error.

During that time, I would sometimes walk on the banks of a lake near Bear Mountain, New York. One day, as I gazed out across the surface of the lake reflecting the light of the setting sun, I asked myself, "What should I do?" What occurred to me then was that I should get to know the US inside and out. I felt that I really needed to experience the US for myself, with my own two eyes and feet.

I decided to get a car and travel across the country from east to west. Our itinerary would take us from New York to California, along the western coast up to Vancouver, through Toronto, and then back to New York. For several months, I wandered through the beautiful mountains and valleys of the US. I went inside the busy metropolitan areas as well, and felt the confusion of their people's hearts. It was a good opportunity for me to feel the energy of this massive land with my own body, mind, and senses.

As I crossed the country, there was one thing I was looking for: a new land where I could put down my roots and thrive. The moment I saw Sedona, I felt a strong intuition that this would be that very place. However, although I stayed in Sedona for three days, I was still unable to make a final decision.

One of the reasons I hesitated was that Sedona was a desert. According to the Eastern practice of *feng shui*, a harmony of the five energies—wood, fire, earth, metal, and water—is essential.

Certainly, wood energy was coming from the forests of juniper trees and shrubs; there was obviously plenty of fire energy since it was a desert where the sun beat down strongly; judging by the power pouring from the ground of Sedona, nothing needed to be said about earth energy; and since it was iron that gave to the earth its deep red color, it was also full of metal energy. However, since it was a desert terrain where water was scarce, the thought that water energy might be insufficient kept bothering me.

I went back to Los Angeles and returned to Sedona after a few days. It was then I saw something that blew away all my concerns—Oak Creek Canyon, where the creek flowed right alongside the highway going up from Sedona to Flagstaff. During my first visit I couldn't see it closely, but there was clear water flowing abundantly through the canyon. I realized then that Sedona had the necessary amount of water energy, too. With this in mind, I found a desire to make a new start in Sedona where, although it was desert terrain, the energy of the five elements were harmonized so well. And I started to feel certain that, in a place like this, I could establish the meditation center of which I had dreamed.

It took me a few more days to look around the Native American reservations and nearby famous locations in Arizona, Utah, and Nevada. I also visited Lake Powell, Rainbow Bridge, the Grand Canyon, Bryce Canyon, and the canyons of Zion National Park. All of them were places that had not only been regarded as sacred by Native Americans, but also displayed the beauty and dignity of nature without restraint. I was also pleased with the fact that Sedona was not too far from many of these places. Having resolved upon my second visit to move there, I now rented a modest place that I could use as a home and office.

As I drove back to Los Angeles to prepare for my move, I had a premonition that something good was going to happen, and I felt a nervous excitement. I kept repeating the name of the land, "Sedona," over and over in my mind. Se-do-na. Se-do-na. Se . . . do . . . na. Then, all of a sudden, a thought came to my mind: *Se-do-na*, a place where a new Tao or enlightenment would emerge. Viewing these syllables in Korean, "Se" sounds like "sae" and means "new," "do" means "Tao" or "enlightenment," and "na" means "is coming out." If you put the three parts together, then Sedona means "the land where a new enlightenment will emerge."

From that point onward, every time I pronounced Sedona's name, every time I told other people about Sedona, and every time I practiced meditation in Sedona, I started to believe that a new enlightenment would arise from this place. That was my belief and it was also my profound hope. And this is how my Sedona story began.

2 A LAND OF YEARNINGS AND DREAMS

EVERY LAND HAS A sacred mountain or a place of wonder where people gather, drawn by the extraordinary energy there. Sedona is no different. I have traveled to many sacred places around the world, including those in India, Nepal, Israel, South America, and Europe, but I have yet to encounter a place that draws the heart as does Sedona. This is already the fifteenth year that I've been living here, but the red rocks and sunsets that I see here still move my heart in a continually fresh way.

Sedona is a small city in the center of Arizona, a state located in the desert of the southwestern United States. It's about two hours by car from the Grand Canyon and about 120 miles north of Phoenix, Arizona's capital. It's often referred to as "red rock country" because of its monumental landscape of red rock. As you enter the city, you'll see why locals like to say, "God created the Grand Canyon, but He lives in Sedona."

One might assume that Sedona is a place of sweltering heat because of its desert location, but in fact there are four beautiful seasons. In the spring, the dry fields are blanketed with wildflowers. In the fall, the leaves turn and flood the Oak Creek Canyon with orange and golden yellow foliage. Winter is equally beautiful in Sedona. The sight of fluffy white snow piling softly on the red rocks is exquisite; and when the snow stops falling and the sun comes out, the red rocks, green cacti, and blue sky radiate their own dazzling light. When you see such sights, you understand why people call Sedona "The City of Light," and you find yourself nodding your head in agreement.

Though Sedona has a population of about 10,000 people, more than three million tourists come here each year. However, unlike the usual tourist locations, Sedona is a very quiet city. Most of the restaurants and stores close by 9:00 p.m. It's a city that couldn't be more boring for people who are looking for nightlife. But for people who know the joy of communing with nature, it's a place that often gives them the irresistible urge to pack their things and move here at once. Actually, a considerable number of Sedona residents first came as tourists and fell in love with the place.

Sedona was registered as a city in 1902, taking its name from the wife of the white settler who was head of the first post office. According to archaeologists who research ancient Native Americans sites, the Native Americans who lived in

northern Arizona for thousands of years have long regarded Sedona and its surrounding Oak Creek Canyon as an especially sacred place. The Native American sites discovered here are not centered on Sedona; instead they encircle it. The Native Americans visited Sedona only when they were conducting rituals or religious ceremonies. Even today, just as Hindus make a pilgrimage to the Ganges River, several Yavapai and Apache tribes come to Sedona to perform traditional ceremonies and blessings.

Sedona is also a haven for artists and art lovers. It hosts some forty art galleries. From galleries to studios, art is everywhere in this small town. Sedona is truly the perfect city for artistic inspiration. In Sedona, everyone naturally feels the urge to paint a picture or play a flute. Standing before a display of the beautiful artistry of nature, human beings want to dance and sing and demonstrate their own creativity as well. Although I had never played music, even I learned to play the flute and do calligraphy here.

One of the things you can never leave out when speaking about Sedona are its vortexes. A vortex describes the energy field of an object rotating in a spiral around a central axis. Examples include a tornado, or water forming a whirlpool as it goes down a drain. Actually, from the smallest atoms to the Milky Way, we find that our universe is full of vortexes.

Vortex sites in Sedona are powerful energy spots that facilitate self-awareness and various healing experiences. They say the red iron rocks generate this kind of energy, as well as the massive crystals buried beneath them. Bell Rock, Airport Mesa, Cathedral Rock, and Boynton Canyon are known as four major vortexes. But in my experience, it's not just these four places; Sedona itself *is* a vortex. Every time I return to it, I am surprised to feel how much energy is here.

The Native Americans called Sedona "the land where Mother Earth's energy, which gives eternal life, comes out." Furthermore, they believed that "great souls" inhabit the red rocks, and that they make the people who come and find Sedona awaken to their true dreams and yearnings.

I believe these legends are not merely wishful thinking. That's because I, too, have met with great souls from the red rocks of Sedona, and have cultivated here my yearnings and dreams.

3 ONLY ONE QUESTION

AFTER MOVING TO SEDONA, the first thing I did was walk around every inch of it until my feet had blisters. Granted, I have always had a lot of curiosity and a love of adventure, as well as a perennial inability to be satisfied with anything less than experiencing everything for myself, but the more I discovered Sedona's mysterious appeal, the more it called me to its rocky mountains every day.

Perhaps word had gotten out that I was searching out its uncharted areas because, one day, a person came to me saying that he knew all of Sedona's terrain. He said he had it in his head in greater detail than if it were written down on a map. He was a "vortex guide" who was half Caucasian and half Native American. I began exploring the area with him. Starting with the four famous vortexes, I examined every nook and cranny of Sedona over the course of several weeks until there was no spot I hadn't visited.

This guide, who had a merry and outgoing disposition and played the flute quite well, came to me one day and said, "There's a saying, 'When you come to Sedona, you have to set aside all of your personal thoughts and desires. If you don't, you can't receive Sedona's energy, and furthermore you could pollute Sedona.' That's why you have to clear your mind and prepare yourself before you come."

I nodded in agreement. "That's right, since you can't fill something if you don't empty it first. Then how can you set down your thoughts and desires?"

The guide shrugged his shoulders, as if to say he wasn't really sure. I showed him how to awaken the sense of energy in his body and empty his mind to become one easily with nature. And before our journey together concluded, I made sure to tell him, "Why don't you listen to your inner self sometimes, in silence? When you're inside of that quietude, you can interact more deeply with Sedona's energy. Then you won't just be a person who shares the beautiful outer trails; you'll become a guide who helps people to cultivate the trails of their lives and make them beautiful, too."

He thought about my advice for a moment, and then suddenly asked with a sincere expression, "It seems like you're some kind of expert . . . What do you do?"

What do I do? What, I wondered, would be a good way to introduce myself to this person? When he asked me that question, the many things that I had experienced before coming to Sedona came to my mind. Depending on what was needed, I had played many different roles and worn many different hats in order to fulfill my dreams.

But though I'd had many names and titles, there had always been only one question behind everything I had done. That question was, "Who am I?" Who was I *really*?

4 My Early Days in Korea

I WAS BORN IN December 1950, amidst the fires of the Korean War. When I was young, I was unusually soft-hearted and physically weak. I encountered many difficulties because I couldn't focus well on my studies at school. That was not only because my body was weak, but also because demanding questions like, "Why am I here?" wouldn't leave me alone, and I couldn't focus on what I was supposed to be learning.

Naturally, my academic record was downright awful, and on more than one occasion, I embarrassed my father, who was the vice-principal at the elementary school that I attended. It was no fun playing with other kids my age, so I rambled around a nearby mountain by myself and picked wild fruit to eat or leaned against the trunk of a pine tree and let my mind wander in daydreams. Every so often, I would wonder, "Why am I here?" or I would have the thought that being trapped inside my body felt too stuffy and confining.

During one summer vacation at age fourteen, I was involved in a tragic accident when I went swimming in the reservoir with a friend and he drowned. Because of the shock and grief I felt, I was sick in bed for nearly a month afterward and experienced acute fear and anxiety about death. The thought that someday, like my friend, my parents and I and everything in the world would disappear made life seem pointless. The barrier between me and my academic studies became even greater, and I had no place to put my mind. So every day, for hours on end, I practiced martial arts such as taekwondo and hapkido.

In high school, I became an extreme existentialist. I asked my friends, "Hey, why do you live?" and I would often say, "People live to die," and sneer at people who were living diligently and quietly. I would often look up at the night sky and protest in a voice rife with indignation, "God, if you put me on this world without bothering to get my permission, shouldn't you at least tell me why I should live?" Those were days of terrible frustration. I felt a resentment that wasn't directed toward anyone in particular, and I was bursting with questions that had no answers.

At twenty-two, I belatedly became a college student and studied clinical pathology and physical education. After I graduated, I got married, worked as the head of pathology in a good hospital, and I made a real effort to live diligently as a steady breadwinner and head of the household.

I fathered two sons and had a stable lifestyle, but on the way home from work every day, if I looked up at the sky, I would feel a sudden rush of sadness and an intense loneless that would well up inside me all the way to my throat. From the outside, my life didn't look like it had any problems, but it was difficult to endure as time passed by without my having any greater sense of what the meaning of my life really was.

That was when I started wandering about in search of someone who could give me the answer to the issues of life and death . . . or at least offer some clues! I looked for and found books about philosophy and the spiritual world, and every time I had a chance, I would seek out people who were said to have performed ascetic practices in the mountains. If I even heard a rumor about someone who had studied those issues extensively, I would toss my work aside and chase after them. But I couldn't find anything that resonated within me, and the pointlessness and suffering I felt only kept growing.

5 THE HUNDRED-DAY TRAINING

ONE DAY IN THE LATE 1970S, I made my way to an antique bookstore in Cheonggyecheon in Seoul. It was a place I had visited often in search of books about martial arts, ki (chi) energy, Tao, and Eastern medicine. I was glancing around the bookshelves when a book caught my eye. It had been partially burned and half the cover had fallen off. I reached for it absentmindedly. It was a book about tai chi. I opened the book to somewhere in the middle, and as soon as I did, the words, "He who masters ki energy through Tao will have no enemies in all the world," jumped out at me.

That instant, I was shocked by a current of powerful energy running through my body as if I had been electrocuted, and I felt a shiver and shudder go through my whole body. From then on, I wasn't the one who was moving my body. Instead, some powerful energy started to move within me.

I went to sleep that night resolved to wake up early the next morning at 4:00 a.m., and when I opened my eyes, it was exactly 4:00 a.m. Rather than saying, "I got up," it would be more accurate to say that my body got up on its own and went to the nearby mountain to train. From that time on, my life took a 180-degree turn. I was living inside of the ki energy, flowing with the ki energy, and drunk with the ki energy.

The instant I thought of reading something, my hand would reach out to where the book was; even when I was eating, the energy would lift my hand to pick up my spoon. Just like astronauts floating around in zero gravity, I felt like my body didn't require the use of any strength or effort, and it moved around by itself automatically. Sometimes, everything seemed to be happening very slowly, as though

I were watching a video in slow motion. But that's not to say that I was in a dreamlike state; my awareness remained very clear.

I didn't want to lose this incredible feeling, so I resolved to train for one hundred days. This hundred-day training just happened without effort. At 4:00 a.m., my eyes would open on their own, and before I knew it, I was sitting on the nearby mountain. My feet would stop on their own at a certain spot. When I sat down and steadied my breath, the ki energy circulated throughout my body and a pillar of light came down in front of me; in it I saw a person shining with a golden light. If I opened my eyes and got up, the golden light would disappear. I didn't realize it until later, but the light was coming from my own body.

Strangely enough, no matter how long I sat, I wasn't tired. My breathing became so deep that I could barely tell if I was breathing at all. If I just sat down, all the weight of my body disappeared. My hands would float up automatically and perform movements I had never learned that seemed like martial arts and also like dancing. I could hear my pulse, loud as the sound of a drum, and I even heard the blood flowing in my body as if it were the rushing waters of a stream after a torrential rain.

At that time, something extraordinary also happened professionally. As soon as I saw the faces of the patients who came to my clinical pathology office, the numbers for their blood pressure or blood sugar levels came to my mind; later, when I performed the tests, their results would match those numbers exactly. At that time, I understood such experiences to be the result of the ki energy training, but I still didn't know the principles behind it.

Toward the end of the hundred-day training period, I had an important experience that made me realize the power of the energy latent in a human being. During a news broadcast one night, I heard that the temperature the next day would be twenty degrees below zero Celsius. I wondered if, with that kind of extreme cold, I would have to take a break from my training. I couldn't give up on it, if only because of the sincere devotion I had given it so far, so I left the house in the morning as usual.

But once up the mountain, I realized that I had underestimated the cold. As soon as I sat down on the snowy rock, my whole body began to shiver so much that I simply couldn't focus my mind. Even the golden light figure that I could usually see if I closed my eyes didn't appear.

As time went by, I felt my body freezing. Even my tears were frozen. When the cold became unbearable, I started to worry. I thought, "If my body just freezes like this, I'm in trouble." But I didn't want to give up. A certain kind of defiant stubbornness rose up in me. "If Heaven wants to take me because my time's up, then there's nothing I can do about it. I can't live just because I want to, and I can't just die because I want to. Let's put everything in Heaven's hands and observe what it's like to freeze to death."

I lowered my shoulders, which were tensed up high from the cold, and tried to gather ki energy in my lower belly and breathe. But it was so cold that my body would only keep shaking and I couldn't breathe deeply. It seemed that my body was slowly becoming paralyzed and even my mind was becoming half-conscious. That's when it occurred to me that I had really made the wrong decision. I thought, "I'd better stop before it's too late," and I hastily tried to get up. But it *already* was too late. My body had become paralyzed. I couldn't budge.

Waves of regret washed over me. And what came to me next was an uncontrollable fear. I was swallowed up by a fear of death. I struggled and made my most desperate effort to move, but my body had become as stiff as a rock. I had reached that moment when I had to give up on "life and death"—whether I wanted to or not. As I resigned myself to my fate, I said, "Oh Heaven . . . please do as you see fit."

And that's when something amazing happened. Suddenly, my breathing became comfortable and my lower belly started getting warmer. Something in my lower belly loosened and began to move, and then the energy center in my lower belly got very hot and its heat began to surge throughout my body with an almost explosive force. I wondered, "Did the primal energy in my body become activated by the dire situation?" I watched this phenomenon unfold inside me. Clouds of steam were rising off my body as the sweat poured from it. I could see even the snow around me melting.

Then my whole body shook as it started bouncing up and down. It was a violent sort of shaking. I was seated in the lotus posture and trembling as though I were an aspen leaf when, all of a sudden, I floated up high and then dropped to the ground. In that instant, it felt like the joints of my arms and legs had all popped out and then worked their way smoothly back into their proper places.

I stood up. My body was unspeakably hot. It grew as hot as a lump of coal and an incredible strength burst forth from inside it that I couldn't restrain. There was so much energy flowing out of me that I didn't know what to do, and before I knew it, I had pulled up a smallish pine tree with my hand. How strong are the roots of a pine tree in the winter? But the tree that had been stuck in the frozen ground came out easily, roots and all. This is what occurs when the energy circulation in our body becomes perfect and we are able to use our extreme power.

Although the hundred-day period was over, my training still hadn't come to an end. Soon it was day one hundred one . . . then day one hundred two. My training grew deeper and even more intense. Then, one day, I felt with desperate certainty a need to leave my job and family for a while and really make a time and space in which I could focus on myself one hundred percent in order to find the answer to the ultimate question of life. Thus, after making preparations so that my family would not have to worry about their livelihood, I turned my steps to a place that I had received guidance about through an inspiration during my early morning training several months earlier. That place was Moak Mountain in a southern part of South Korea.

6 Twenty-one Days on Moak Mountain

IN JUNE OF 1980, I arrived at a small Buddhist temple called Donggoksa, which is located halfway up Moak Mountain. I had made up my mind to focus on training for twenty-one days without eating, sleeping, or lying down. That's because, through the experience of my hundred-day training, I had come to have faith that if I gave my sincere devotion to an extreme situation, a strength other than my own would come to guide me and lift me up.

At first, I went up from the bottom of Moak Mountain to Donggoksa and back down three times a day. My body was so light, it seemed to be flying. Around the third day, I was still able to endure the hunger by drinking water, but the problem was the sleepiness that came pouring down on me. I walked through the mountain even at night to stave off the fatigue. There were times when I had to keep walking just to stay awake, and I even stood for several hours holding onto a pine tree.

Around the fifth day, my eyelids were very heavy and it was hard to keep my eyes open. I really knew what was meant by the saying that the heaviest things in the world are your eyelids when you're sleepy. The sleepiness was so overwhelming that, even when I was standing, my legs would falter. Next to Donggoksa, there was a small waterfall. In order to endure the sleepiness, I would sit kneeling at the edge of the cliff where the waterfall started. I thought that the sense of tension I felt from knowing that I would get hurt if I got drowsy and fell would act as a stimulant to keep the drowsiness at bay. Even so, I became drowsy enough to fall down the cliff. What's more, it happened three times. But the amazing thing is that, aside from a few bruises, I was fine.

During my twenty-one day training, in a state of super-consciousness that went beyond the world of the five senses, I had many energetic and spiritual experiences. I didn't sleep, but if I think about it now, I was in an almost half-asleep state. However, although my body was in a half-asleep state, my consciousness was lucid.

When I closed my eyes, sometimes writing came down from heaven, or visions of various sages, saints, and enlightened masters that I had read about would appear and give me this message or that. Sometimes I would see in advance who would come up the mountain the next day, or I could see plainly before my eyes the happenings in the valley at the foot of Moak Mountain, or what was happening in my faraway home. Sitting at the top of Moak Mountain, I was even able to see the fish swimming around the lake at the foot of the mountain.

It was approaching the end of the twenty-one day training. I had a headache and the pain was difficult to bear. It hurt so much it felt like my head would break. It was so painful that I could barely stay conscious. Even my eyes and ears hurt so much that I could neither see nor hear. I heard a creaking, breaking sound as if the bones of my head were stretching or something. I thought I just might die from my head exploding. I thought my eyeballs would burst, and suddenly my nose starting bleeding profusely. I think it was because all the energy had flooded my head. I tried all sorts of things to try to bring the energy back down. I tried jumping up and down with all my strength, and I tried doing headstands. I also tried pressing on my neck. I even tried hitting my head against a rock. But it was useless. The pain didn't decrease even a little bit. I don't know how much time went by like that. My sense of time had already vanished.

Finally, I gave up all effort. I thought, "If my head has to be smashed for this pain to go away, then fine, let it be smashed." It took all my effort but I sat down once again in the lotus posture. I controlled my breathing and, with great effort, maintained composure and observed the intense pain. That instant, a thought brushed by me like a flash of lightning. "Who is feeling pain? Yes, the one in pain is only my head. My head—that's not me. My head is just part of my body, it's not me. My body is simply mine, it's not me." At that instant, a realization like a flash of light exploded in my brain that cut away all thought and preconceptions that were limitations created by my body. Suddenly, I heard a sound in my head like a huge explosion.

"Boom!"

I thought that instant was the end of my life. But I was alive. It felt like my head had gone, so I lifted my hand and felt for it. My head was still there and my headache was gone instead.

All pain disappeared and everything was peaceful. That peace was so immense. It felt like the skin that had separated my body from its surroundings had disappeared. It was one instant. Everything became clear. The place of my inner Self that completely transcends time and space, a place of complete freedom and peace where everything is integrated as one . . . *this was it!* I encountered an indescribable moment of brightness that cleared away all the dark clouds at once.

At that moment, a voice inside me asked, "Who am I?" The answer from inside of me came with utter confidence, "I am Chunjikiun (cosmic energy). I am Chunjimaum (cosmic mind)." This energy that fills the universe is me. Though I was born of my parents, Heaven and Earth, actually I was never born. What was born was my body, simply my physical form. I existed before I received this body. I am the eternal and fundamental life energy of the universe. The music of the universe reverberated in my heart and the breath of nature went in and out through my skin. The universe and I were not separate, and nature and myself were not two. I am the center of heaven and earth. Everything is one. One!

7 AFTER ENLIGHTENMENT

A FTER COMPLEING THE TWENTY-ONE DAY training on Moak Mountain, I stayed for another twenty-one days. The first few days, I remained speechless inside the infinite brightness. There was nothing else I could do but exist in the silence. However, after a few days, I started to become concerned. What was I supposed to do now? What would I do with my enlightenment?

After deliberating for a few days more, I saw, during meditation, a vision of the earth shining beautifully blue and green. I was watching with wonder and admiration when, suddenly, the earth approached me at a frightening speed. I breathed in sharply because of the immense impact of the energy. The earth was so close it was almost touching me.

I reached out my hands and caressed the earth with my palms. My breath blended with the earth's breath, and we breathed as one. The feeling of love was so strong that I felt like I had never loved anyone as I loved the earth in that moment.

The next moment, the earth began slowly turning in front of me. I could feel the continents and great oceans of the earth passing beneath my palms. Then it fell away from me very quickly at an alarming speed.

After that, innumerable visions flashed by in front of my eyes. The images were of two kinds. The first was of humanity suffering tragically from natural disasters, wars, and disease. The spectacle was so horrible that it made me shudder. The other set of images was very different. They were of all people and even nature living in health, happiness, and peace. The contrast between the horror and the beauty were so strong that, at that moment, the fate of humanity became my fate; it dug into my heart and became something my soul could never shake off again.

I had found my life's work. To contribute to changing humanity's fate to happiness and peace—this was my mission. My inner Self was shouting at me to run toward that great mission, and that doing that work was the reason for my existence. This voice was so loud and so earnest that I couldn't turn away. That's why I have to do what I do.

But how in the world would I do this? What ability did I have that would make me capable? There wasn't anybody in the world who had asked me to do this work. *Who would want me to do this?* I wondered.

All I could do was encourage myself. As long as I felt

that this work was my life, it didn't matter what people thought of me.

I made my body get up. *Let's give it a go.* People aren't going to come to me. I have to go to where the people are. *Come on, let's go.* Let's share this awakening that I've attained with others. If I don't know the way, I'll ask as I go, and if I ask but there's no path, then I just need to make one and take it. These were the resolutions I made as I came down from Moak Mountain.

Before I had left for Moak Mountain, I had started a spring water company. That was because I felt that even if I went to the mountain, I had to assure my family's livelihood. When I came back from Moak Mountain, however, the water company had gone broke, and my family was experiencing financial difficulties. Faced with that reality, I was completely at a loss for what to do and where to start.

How paradoxical was it? In the spiritual world, I had nothing more to seek. For someone who had experienced oneness with the universe, the earth looked as small as a bean. But the economic reality in front of my eyes was disheartening.

The gap between the spiritual and the material world looked more like a chasm. So what did that make my enlightenment? Did that mean my enlightenment—which I could feel so clearly even now—was no more than a delusion? And what did that make me, concerned as I was by the present reality? This is when I had the acute realization that spreading my enlightenment in the physical world wouldn't be such an easy task after all.

Where would I start, with what, and how? One thing was certain: the only way to confirm whether what I had attained was real or not would be to try to communicate it. If people weren't inspired and nothing changed after I conveyed my enlightenment, then I would know I had been mistaken. But if my enlightenment was communicated to others who could also feel the Chunjikiun and Chunjimaum I had felt, then wouldn't my enlightenment be beneficial not only to me but to others as well?

I got up early the next morning and went to the park. I wanted to meet people and try sowing the new seeds. The first person I met at was an elderly gentleman who had had a stroke. He was exercising, and I could see from the way he was moving that it was uncomfortable for him; I approached him and massaged his shoulders and back and taught him some exercises that he could do easily. After a couple of more days, the number of people started to increase. People who had been hanging around watching our strange move-ments, people who were trying to catch a glimpse of what we were doing from a safe distance away and even trying to follow along, even people who came after hearing rumors of what we were doing, soon joined us. It wasn't long before there were well over ten people training with me early every morning.

Around that time, too, the first draft of the design for testing my truth came to me. In the midst of teaching and speaking with the people I had met at the park, I thought deeply about ways that I could better communicate my enlightenment. That's when I realized my enlightenment came from the lineage of philosophy of the Sundo culture, a Korean Taoist tradition with a 10,000-year history. Thus, I modernized the traditional Korean mind-body training methods that were based on Sundo and organized them into a system of training called Dahnhak. That's when I had the idea to open centers where these training methods could be taught; thus, I opened a small space of nine hundred square feet. That was the very first Dahn Center.

But even to reach this point was not easy. Enlightenment was only the beginning. What changed after my enlightenment was my own consciousness; my surroundings remained exactly the same. I had the dream, but I had no way of knowing how or what to do to achieve that dream. I had no experience or anyone to help me, but I chose to trust in Heaven and just do it. It took me five years of going to the park where I would teach people, talk about my dream, and meet those people who would join me in that dream.

Until I came to Sedona, for ten years I poured my body and soul into sharing Dahnhak in Korea. I continued my studies to find ways to more easily awaken the inner greatness and infinite potential in more people, and I developed many training methods. I authored books, cultivated students, toured the major cities, and delivered public lectures. What had started with the one nine hundred square foot location had expanded to fifty locations by the time I came to Sedona.

8 THE SEDONA MEDITATION TOUR

EVEN AFTER SCOUTING the vortexes of Sedona for several weeks with that tour guide, I kept investigating all the nooks and crannies in the mountains and valleys. During meditation, if I got the intuition, "that's the mountain for today," as soon as daybreak arrived, that's where I headed. I went up the rocky mountains even in the middle of the night, and when I was passing a place in the car, if I felt it was calling me, I would park by the roadside and walk up the mountain trails. I felt it was a shame to sit in these beautiful and inspiring places by myself, so I called the students who were close to me and they went with me, too.

As I practiced meditation alone in the mountains and valleys of Sedona, as well as with my students, I naturally came to combine my experiences of Sedona's vortex energy with the Dahn Yoga energy principles and training methods

I had taught over the years. I taught how to live one's life with a sense of true ownership by utilizing its principles.

In the human body, there are meridians, the paths along which our energy flows, and there are acupressure points, which are the openings where energy comes in and out. Also, there are invisible energy centers where energy is concentrated. These are called "chakras" in the Indian tradition and are referred to as "dahnjons" in the Korean Sundo tradition.

Because the earth is also an organic life form, it has an energy system similar to that of the human body. Vortexes perform a similar role for the earth as chakras do for the human body. Power is concentrated in the vortexes; the energy of the earth pours out in swirling spirals or the energy of heaven comes to them and forms a whirling spiral. Just as the energy of our bodies is not visible to the naked eye, vortex energy is also invisible. However, just as you can feel energy if you focus your mind, it's possible to experience vortex energy through our various senses.

The vortex energy of Sedona has the power to correct the energy imbalance in the human chakras. The instant the energy vortexes in our body meet Sedona's energy vortexes, damaged systems can revert to their original balanced state. However, just because you're in a vortex doesn't necessarily mean that you can experience this phenomenon. Even if you're in a spot where the energy is good, it's no use if you don't know how to feel and utilize this energy.

Furthermore, it's about how you can interact more deeply with nature through this vortex energy and live a healthier and more creative life. Also, it's not about dwelling on the fascinating energy experience itself; it's about being able to go deeper to discover and actualize the great dream and strength inside yourself.

Millions of tourists visit Sedona each year, but how many of them actually get the inspiration they need? The majority of these people come because they're drawn to this place, but to me it felt like a shame to see only Sedona's beautiful landscape.

I decided to try something new. It was to combine journeying with meditation and to start a self-development program called the Sedona Meditation Tour. The Sedona Meditation Tour created a huge sensation. My students in Korea who had missed me while I had been active mainly in the US, and those who had read my words, started coming to Sedona to meet with me. The students in other areas of the US also started to come to Sedona. It made my heart skip a beat to think about meeting them in Sedona, this beautiful and sacred land.

I scoured every inch of Sedona and went on practically every trail. There were times when I clambered up steep mountains where there was no trail at all, when it was hard to find my way back home because the sun had gone down, or, if I saw a rocky summit, when I would get curious about what the view was like and, not having a place to put my foot, almost fall. I would make my way around Sedona like that, and if I discovered a place that was so amazing that it called forth an automatic exclamation, the first thing that came to my mind were the faces of my students. My heart would become too full just hinking about us meditating together in this amazing place, talking about nature and life, and about our beautiful dream.

I mainly sought out not only the vortex areas of Sedona, but also the places that the Native Americans regarded as sacred and where they performed their spiritual rituals. When I did the Meditation Tour with people who didn't have much training experience, we went to wellknown vortex areas along easy paths that didn't take us high into the mountain or deep into the valley. However, when I was with people who had a lot of training, we went down into the canyons and stayed for a long time in one place, meditating and sharing in conversation.

Before starting each Meditation Tour, I always would say, "Sedona is beautiful. But your soul is far more beautiful. Please don't just become drunk on Sedona's beauty, but open your ears to your inner self. Then you will hear a voice from within. That's the message that Sedona is giving you."

Sedona is a place where it's easy to take down the defensive walls that surround you. In our interpersonal relationships, we can't open ourselves up one hundred percent. People are so busy trying to protect themselves that they create a defensive shield that's not always visible. By defensive shield, I mean something that becomes an obstacle to interacting with other people because of a "closed" heart; it also blocks the energy of Mother Nature coming into our own body. Inside of a defensive shield like that, one cannot look deeply into the self. The beautiful and magnificent landscape of Sedona and its wide open, unrestrained energy clears away that shield for you very naturally. When this shield is dropped, the true meditation tour that goes to the inner self begins.

The combination of meditation and journeying is an especially effective method for developing our brain. Travels that take us away from our everyday lives let our bodies and minds relax, while at the same time they awaken our minds to the anticipation of new experiences. This easily facilitates a state of "relaxed concentration" that provides those conditions that enable us to access the maximum power of our brain.

If you add meditation, the effect is enhanced. The combination of meditation and journey here in Sedona, a place that uplifts our consciousness with its special energy and activates the energy circulation inside the human body, greatly amplifies the power of this process.

9 THE ROCKS AND HILLS OF SEDONA THAT I LOVE

THE NEXT FEW CHAPTERS are about the mountains, valleys, and rocks of Sedona that I climbed either by myself, with my students, or with the people who came on the Meditation Tour. They're also about the mind of the earth as conveyed to me by Sedona's mountains and fields. As we climb up mountains, look at the flowers and trees, and gaze out across lakes, we feel the beauty of nature. However, it's usually more of us thinking, "That mountain is beautiful," or "The sky is lovely," or "This place is so peaceful." Rarely do we encounter a place that gives us the feeling that, "This Earth is beautiful." I really got that feeling quite a lot in Sedona. Perhaps it is because it's a place where you can see the beauty of heaven and earth at once, but every time I came here, the whole of the earth came into my heart.

AIRPORT MESA

If you were to ask me to name the vortex area easiest to approach, it would definitely be Airport Mesa. If you leave by car from Uptown Sedona, you can arrive in five minutes and, as soon as you get out, you enter the vortex. It's ideal for people for whom hiking or mountain climbing is difficult. This place, which is as flat as if the top of the mountain had been sheared off, actually has an airport on it so smaller airplanes and helicopters can take off and land.

Because it's right in the middle of town, you can see all of Sedona at a glance. There are two overlooks that people mainly visit: one of them is at the top on the right when you drive to the summit and the other is a mini-mesa located to the left, about halfway up Airport Road.

If you stand on top of the mini-mesa, a captivating view of Sedona spreads out before you like a panorama that starts with Bell Rock and Courthouse Butte toward the southwest; Lee Mountain and Munds Mountain to the east; Steamboat, Coffee Pot, Capitol Butte, and Chimney Rock to the north; and Cockscomb and Mingus Mountain in the west. You can see all of them just by standing in one spot and turning your body. This place is like a natural lookout for the city of Sedona because from here you can see its structure in a short time. You just can't see in the direction of Cathedral Rock because it's hidden by one of Airport Mesa's mountaintops. However, if you want to take the time to see all 360 degrees,

you can leave from the mini-mesa and walk along the Airport Mesa Loop Trail that winds clockwise.

The busiest time at Airport Mesa is around sunset. With the onset of evening, crowds of tourists come with cameras in hand to see the sunset. The sunset you see from here makes you understand what's meant by the term "breathtakingly beautiful." On days when there are some low clouds above the western horizon, the sun shoots dazzling rays of white and gold light through the clouds.

When the golden sunlight spreads above the pointy black silhouette of Cockscomb in the direction of the curvy ridges of Mingus Mountain, it looks like the final flourish of golden light painted over an eastern style ink-and-wash painting. The rocks to the east in the same view take the light of the sun, change to a golden color, and then become infused with a more intense, ruddy glow. The whole city is swept up in a magical act of color.

When the sun goes down, the clouds that were radiating golden light gradually melt from orange to vermillion to scarlet to crimson hues until, finally, they fade to ash and then sink into blackness. And night comes to Sedona. Another thing you can't miss at Airport Mesa is stargazing. If you lie down on the rocks that have been warmed up all day by the sun and look up at the night sky, the whole universe comes affectionately close to you.

BELL ROCK

Bell Rock feels like Sedona's mascot. It's the most renowned of Sedona's four major vortexes, so it's a place where tourists are sure to visit at least once. Bell Rock has a very stable form no matter from which direction you see it, and its appearance resembles a well-shaped bell that reminds you of energy that rises up toward heaven.

The road to Bell Rock from the Uptown Sedona area affords a beautiful drive. When I'm coasting along the winding road between forests of low juniper trees and cacti, the red rocks that shoot up beneath the wide open sky seem to run toward me from a distance. From State Route 89A, if you take State Route 179 and drive for about fifteen minutes, you'll see a rock that looks like a bell standing alone on the left; anyone can find it easily.

One reason Bell Rock is so popular is because in its presence it is easy to feel vortex energy. There are people who say they had an experience of powerful energy swirling around and enveloping their whole body, and there are also a number of people who say they've seen moving images that seem to foretell future events.

There is a legend about Bell Rock. A Native American holy man is said to have seen the people suffering while he was praying at the top of it and made the following vow before he died, "Let my bones hold up this rock and let my blood make it red so that I can dwell here forever. Let at least the people who pray here be free from illness and the

suffering and the misery of life." It may be thanks to this legend that Bell Rock is also renowned for powerful healing energy.

A Korean artist in his forties, who had been receiving treatments for years for sciatica, had pain even when walking on flat terrain. He says that even before he went up Bell Rock, he was in pain. As he looked up at the rock, he thought, "If I actually make it up there and back, I probably won't be able to get out of bed tomorrow!" But once he started to climb up Bell Rock, he was surprised to find himself feeling like someone was pulling him up from in front and also pushing him from behind, so it was easy to climb up and down. The next morning, he marveled at how well he felt.

Although it's possible to have many ki energy experiences like this on Bell Rock, that, in itself, is not what's important. The reason I regard training that involves the ki energy as crucial is because ki energy is the bridge that links our body and mind. Through ki energy, you can feel yourself more deeply.

When you focus deeply inside on the ki energy, your mind becomes calm and serene. There's a feeling of peaceful comfort and safety that's hard to describe. Inside of that, there's no fear that you might lose something, there is no desperate need to control others, nor is there the desire for recognition or acceptance. There is only one self that is infinitely bright and peaceful and for which anything seems possible. A precious, holy, and beautiful being: this is how we look as glimpsed through ki energy. However, this being is unfamiliar to a mind that is trapped within preconceptions. That's why we can't think of this being as "me" and why we keep doubting it. That's precisely when we need to talk to our minds. You have to keep reaffirming that that aspect is the *real* you that you had forgotten.

Inside of ki energy, we feel that we are not beings fettered by time and space; instead, we are infinite and eternal. Unlimited peace flows from that eternalness. From time to time, there may be some terror, nervousness, anxiety, fear, or despair that comes to us, but we come to know that that is not all there is. You have to grab hold of that peace that can be felt inside of ki energy. You have to know that the sense of being that seems to extend infinitely without beginning or end is not an illusion. You have to cherish the feeling of that moment and grow and grow it to make it overflow into your whole life. That's when we will not be controlled by the various emotions that come to us or by the ups and downs of life and we will develop the power to control those things. You are then able to embrace all moments of life with confidence and say, "Let joy, sadness, and everything there is come to me."

It's also good to try focusing on ki energy training at Bell Rock. However, do not get caught up only in the energetic sensations themselves, but look deeply into yourself inside of the quiet and peace that those sensations open up for you. Then try sitting halfway up Bell Rock and collecting your breath. Your breathing at that time will be deeper and easier than any breathing you've experienced before then.

When I climb up Bell Rock, I don't think of it simply as climbing a rock. I think of Bell Rock as a human being who has energy and spirit, and I walk with an awareness of where on that human body I'm stepping. Just as there are pathways along which energy flows in the human body, there are channels where the energy circulates in Bell Rock as well. Also, just as there are energy points in the human body where energy goes in and out, Bell Rock also has important energy points. Various locations on Bell Rock each emanate their own unique, characteristic energy.

If you think of the wide, flat, rocky yard that marks the entrance of Bell Rock as the lower belly and the summit as the top of the head, and feel the energy pathways and points as you go up, a deep energy interaction takes place.

Not far from the entrance to Bell Rock, you come upon a wide, flat area. This location is Bell Rock's dahnjon, the energy center in the middle of the lower belly, the second chakra. In the tradition of eastern mind-body training methods, making this dahnjon abundantly full of energy is viewed as the secret to health and happiness. Bell Rock's dahnjon, wide and flat like that of a human being, gives you a very solid, stable feeling.

There are various ways to get to the top of Bell Rock, but in my experience, the best way is as follows. From the northern parking lot of Bell Rock, look toward the path that goes up on the right hand side. I call this path the Immaek

(Conception Vessel Meridian). In eastern medicine, Immaek is the name of an energy pathway that flows along the central line at the front of the human body.

It's truly a marvel that a path to the top has been carved like an engraving on this bell-shaped, bumpy rock mountain. If you go up along this Immaek, its steep angle makes you short of breath, but you get the feeling that you are protected by a certain energy and you feel like you're in your mother's arms. If you go up this path, you come across spots that correspond to Bell Rock's chest and the point where the Immaek ends and the Dokmaek (Governing Vessel Meridian) begins and flows along Bell Rock's back.

It takes about an hour to an hour and a half to make it all the way up to the top of Bell Rock and back. The path to the top is not too hard, but because there are a few tricky spots where you have to crawl up a steep cliff, there aren't many tourists. If you go to the top, it's wide open in all directions so you can look around and see many of the famous rocks in the Sedona area at a glance. It's a magnificent sight.

In order to have an exchange with Bell Rock, we have to first open up our hearts and be pure. The pure, childlike yearning to feel Bell Rock and become one with it has to fill our heart fully. When you have that desire, you can resonate with Bell Rock's energy and Bell Rock will open its invisible spiritual gates. At that time, your experience of Bell Rock will take on a whole new dimension. No matter how often you climb Bell Rock, if you don't have a heart-to-heart connection, your expression will only be, "The view is good, I feel refreshed, this is a workout, and that's about it."

When I was first getting settled in Sedona, I went up and down Bell Rock more than a hundred times. Just as you can feel at certain times the heart of someone you love even without their speaking, I felt Bell Rock's heart. I had the feeling that Bell Rock knew my heart, and I knew its heart. All life is one. That's why life connects with each other. If you connect with Bell Rock, you can send energy to it, and you can also receive energy from it. Thus, a spiritual interaction with Bell Rock becomes possible.

When you go up Bell Rock, imagine that you are stepping on your aged mother's body. The red earth is your mother's flesh, the rocks that stick up are your mother's bones. The cacti and juniper trees are your mother's breath. If we go up with that kind of feeling, our steps could never be rough. Our gratitude becomes deeper and our footsteps become light, as though our body weight has disappeared.

It's rare for people to climb all the way to the top. It's good to go hiking and walk all the way around the middle, or sit and become immersed in thought, or lie down on the broad rocky surface and take a nap. During warm days I recommend taking a sauna on the rocks. This involves lying down on the rock that has been heated by the desert sun, covering your face and arms, and lying there for about fifteen to thirty minutes. The sweat from your back seeps into the hot rock, and the sweat on the front of your body dries in the sunlight and is carried off by the breeze; after fifteen to thirty minutes, your whole body feels light as cotton.

It's wonderful to go around sunset, because you can sit on a platform halfway up Bell Rock and see the sunset coloring the western sky and the golden glow of the rocks as they reflect the setting sun.

CATHEDRAL ROCK

Of the four major vortexes in Sedona, Cathedral Rock is the only one located next to a canyon with flowing water. The clear, pure water of Oak Creek and a forest of sycamores and oak trees enhance the dignity and splendor of this red rock that stands so tall. This place is also one location that photographers favor. It presents some of the most beautiful scenery Sedona has to offer. Here the cameras capture the red shadow of Cathedral Rock that is reflected in a wonderfully clear Oak Creek and surrounded by a beautiful blue sky. Perhaps it's because of the contrast created by the monumental red rock that towers up majestically, but it's a place where the sky looks especially blue, even for Sedona.

Cathedral Rock is a rock that has a variety of faces that change according to your angle of perspective. It's a place of wonder and mystery where, depending on whether you see it at dawn or sunset, or with the moon in the middle of the night, it always looks and feels very different.

The Native Americans referred to Cathedral Rock as the Sun God. It's a name befitting this rock, for it shines especially beautifully at sunrise and sunset. At both times, the sun hangs on a smaller peak situated between two larger peaks. If you go up this small peak, your view of the east and west is unobstructed so that both when the sun goes up and down you can see a beautiful sky. Especially around sunrise, Cathedral Rock in its entirety glows a rosy scarlet. It's an unbelievable color. In order to see the sunrise from Cathedral Rock, it's a good idea to give yourself plenty of time and start climbing the mountain about an hour before the sunrise. At sunset, sit in the middle of Cathedral Rock and watch the sun vanish behind the rock or the forest of oak trees and the light diffusing on the calm surface of the water in the canyon. You feel calm and serene, at peace and cozy.

There's a place where photographers gather at sunset. If you park in the Crescent Moon Ranch parking lot and go to the creek on the right, you can see people with their cameras and tripods as they wait for the sun to set. It's the best place to capture the image of Cathedral Rock, stained even redder in the light of the setting sun and reflected in the surface of the water in the creek. If you keep pressing the camera shutter-release button to capture the landscape, it makes you practically feel like a professional photographer yourself. That's because, with that location and that timing, a beauty and harmony so perfect as to elicit automatic exclamation and praise are achieved no matter who takes the pictures or how they take them.

I usually enjoy meditating as I listen to the sound of the water as I sit on a bank of Oak Creek in the western part of Cathedral Rock. The sound of the running water keeps my ears from getting bored. I do meditations here and go around the rock and follow the trail on the east side to go up Cathedral Rock. When you look up at Cathedral Rock as you follow the trail, it looks much more magnificent and beautiful than when you see it from afar.

It is said that wise Native American elders always made the following request when a member of their family was going to a faraway place. "If you feel like you're growing distant from your soul, come back to your home and go to a sacred mountain. Stay at the mountain until you gain strength from a rock with warm sunlight, wash away the hurt and sadness of the world in a gently flowing stream, and the trees that wave their hands to you like a warm friend will lend you wisdom."

Cathedral Rock must have been one of the sacred mountains of which the Native Americans spoke.

The energy here is very mild. You gently absorb it, like water seeping into parched earth or like melting snow. Rather than being directed outward, the energy soaks inward, so that just by sitting quietly, your mind becomes calm and at ease. Because this soft energy touches your body and mind like a mother's touch, it's a good place for releasing negative emotions or memories.

Emotions are not different from a movie projected on the screen of your mind. People who are stuck deep in their emotions or thoughts are unable to see that it's just a movie. That's why they hang on to their joy and sorrow and are attached to it. In the same way that the screen doesn't disappear when a movie ends, even in the midst of the coming and going of different emotions, there is something in us that doesn't change. There is a being, an existence that watches our nervousness, our sadness, and our loneliness. That's the True Self and the true mind.

We have to learn how to ride the waves of our emotions as if we were surfing, instead of floundering and getting swept up in them. Just as it's important to keep your balance when surfing, you don't get pulled by the undertow of your emotions when you're firmly rooted in your center, which is your True Self. Even in the midst of change, you have to make an effort to see that which doesn't change. We practice meditation for that purpose. Just as one might sit without wavering in the depths of the ocean and watch the waves above you rise and fall with the wind, so one must be detached. Whether things are bad or good, cultivate the "me that watches me."

It's only natural to experience times that are difficult and painful, no matter who you are. Those are times when anyone would feel tempted to give up on their dream. However, if you try to avoid adversity, you'll end up succumbing to the external environment or to your own limitations. You're able to demonstrate the creative wisdom that can overcome the difficulty only if you face it bravely and assertively instead of avoiding it—and you will grow through your hardship.

Why don't you think of it like this: if a hardship comes, an opportunity has come. The time of hardship is also a time when your mind and heart can expand and open. Great hurt can be transformed into great energy. Don't be ashamed to cry. There are tears that fall because of unfairness or sadness, but there are also the tears we shed as our soul looks at us. Do you know those tears? When you tell yourself, "It's okay," your soul finds strength in those simple words. It's just the way it is that our soul finds more strength from the comfort received from itself than from another.

We are able to find true strength and rest only inside of ourselves. Our very body is a sanctuary and a generator of energy. When things are hard and confusing, go inside. The place can provide you with perfect rest. No matter where you go, dragging your body along with you, you cannot find true rest outside of yourself. Sit or lie down comfortably and, as you collect your breath, let your mind observe your body; then tell yourself, "It's okay." That's when your soul becomes at ease and your body also obtains comfort and new strength.

When you sit in front of Cathedral Rock, even before you say a thing, this red mountain is already comforting you, saying, "It's okay, it's okay." There isn't anyone who doesn't obtain strength from the warmth of that mountain.

Schnebly Hill

In Sedona, sunset is the most meditative time of the day. If you're there when the desert sun, which has been scorching as though it would bleach the whole world, gently stains the land and sky, you automatically understand why the Native Americans called this place the Land of Light.

One of the best places to see the sunset in Sedona is Airport Mesa. It's a high, flat area that seems as though it were leveled by a bulldozer and you can see the whole sunset in the western sky. On a summer evening, it's packed with residents who have come for fresh air and with tourists madly shooting away on their cameras.

But the most beautiful sunset I've ever seen was from Schnebly Hill. If you drive up by car for about twenty minutes from the entrance parking lot, you can see a formation called Merry-Go-Round at the left. Grayish apache limestone forms the round base, while the red and orange Schnebly Hill sandstone stands tall and firm in quirky shapes. I used to park at the right on Schnebly Hill Road and climb to the top at the backside of the Merry-Go-Round.

Off to the west, the red rocks such as Coffee Pot Rock, Mitten Ridge, Thumb Butte, and Moose's Butte amaze you with panoramic views, and the front is wide open so you can look down and see downtown Sedona in the distance.

Especially in the summer, there's a moment when the sun is about to go down and it hangs between two rocks that are backlit so that only their dark outlines show. The day's final rays reach between the rocks and fall right where you're standing. I would go to Schnebly Hill on a summer evening just for that sunset that lasted for only a short time.

Before there were highways in Sedona, Schnebly Hill Road was the road farmers and ranchers used to transport their crops and their cows to Flagstaff. Now, it's mainly tourist jeeps or mountain bikers who go on this path. It's a beautiful trail that glows in the sunset with colors that change from one moment to the next.

Below, there are three wide rock formations that seem bigger than stadiums. These rocks, which could easily seat several thousand people, are called Cow Pies because, from the air, they are shaped like cow dung. Of course, they were named that based on their shape, but the feeling they give me is much more sacred, so I gave them the name Hanmadang Rock. "Han" means "big and wide," but it also means the "one," the "Tao." "Madang" means "ground."

When I stood on this rock and looked up at the surrounding red rocks and the sky, I saw an image of Native Americans gathered to offer a ceremony to heaven. I came to know that this is a sacred place where Native American tribes had held ancestral ceremonies. Before I came to this rock with others, I respectfully asked its spirit, "May I come here to meditate with my students? Will you give me permission?" I received the message that we would be welcome, and I was overjoyed.

I would climb up Schnebly Hill late in the afternoon and look at the sunset and down at Sedona where the lights were coming on one by one in the darkness. Afterward, I would come down to Hanmadang Rock and perform a ceremony in which I offered a prayer of gratitude to heaven.

Among the people who came here with me for meditation, there were many who saw vivid images of past lives as Native Americans.

A married couple who had a large business in Korea visited Sedona. The wife, who even at a glance resembled a Native American, said she had the following experience at Hanmadang Rock.

"Even before I came to Sedona, when I practiced meditation, I would glimpse the form of a Native American warrior. A young man who seemed noble was looking down at the valleys and mountains from a rock, but he seemed so purposeless and powerless. I wondered, 'Why did I see something like this?' and I thought about that image several times. I had often heard people around me say that my face resembled that of a Native American, and I had also really liked movies, dolls, and other stuff about those people.

But when I went up Schnebly Hill in Sedona, I suddenly had the feeling, 'Ah, this is the place!' as tears began streaming down my face. I had such a vivid sensation that the rock that I had seen in meditation was Hanmadang Rock, and that field below was where I had fallen to my death. The tribe that I belonged to had lived peacefully in harmony with nature, but because it was weak, it lost a war and so I had come to my death.

That's when I understood why I was focused so tenaciously on the success of my business. I wanted power. I wanted to attain material power with my business. Through this experience, I came to understand the motivation deep in my heart. I resolved to keep working with my husband and making our business flourish, and to use the material success that I had gained to help the growth of consciousness of many people."

Nights are long in Sedona. If you lie down on Hanmadang Rock and look at the sky, the stars pour down into your heart.

If you have a dream in your heart that beats with the pulse of the night sky, then your soul is happy. Even if it's not beneath the stars of Sedona, it could be anywhere on this Earth Star, a soul that has a dream that makes its heart sing is beautiful.

10 THE STORIES THAT SEDONA'S CANYONS TOLD ME

OAK CREEK CANYON

The trees of the desert have few leaves, and cacti stay green throughout the year, so it's not easy to experience autumn in the desert. But autumn in Sedona is different. That's because there's Oak Creek Canyon. This place is a thirteen-mile gorge along a river located inside of Coconino National Park between Flagstaff and Sedona.

If you're driving on the 89A going past Uptown Sedona to Flagstaff in October, let yourself be charmed by the beautifully colored autumn leaves of Oak Creek. Moreover, with the red, fantastically shaped cliffs and green pines and juniper trees as their background, the yellow and red autumn leaves are even more spectacular. When the powerful sunlight of the desert terrain shines through the clear, crisp air

of Coconino National Park, the leaves of its abundant oak trees sparkle like golden jewels.

As you enter Oak Creek Canyon, the very first thing that welcomes you is the forest fragrance. Here, deciduous trees line the trails and the canyon has water so abundant that it's hard to believe you were in desert terrain moments ago. On a summer morning when the leaves are thick, the sunlight shining through their leaves couldn't be more peaceful. In autumn, the dark basalt, gold, and red leaves that have fallen on the clear surface of the water create a beautiful expanse of color. If you walk along the canyon and then look up, the bright blue sky seems to pull you in and, if you turn your head in either direction, red rock cliffs welcome you.

If you drive about seven miles north from Sedona, you will see Slide Rock State Park on the left. It gets its name from a thirty-foot-long creek bed of rock that serves as a natural water slide. In the summer, this creek with water cold as ice is the best summer retreat. This area was originally an apple orchard but became a national park in 1987. Even now, when autumn comes, the fragrance of apples from a few remaining apple trees permeates the air.

In the summer, the best thing you can do is to play in the water here at Slide Rock—just play to your heart's content like a little child. As you splash around, going down the slide, it seems like all the grime comes off your mind. Being focused and fully engaged in play is also a good meditation. It would seem like a very easy one, but there are a lot of people who can't play well because being dignified is ingrained in them. After a time like this where you run around and play in nature like a child, everyone's face becomes bright as a peony.

Sitting under a rock or tree that you like at Oak Creek Canyon and listening to the sound of the water is also a good meditation. While listening to the sound of the water, your mind effortlessly becomes comfortable and calm.

I love the streams of water that gurgle and shout robustly as they flow. They symbolize an aspect of life that always has hope and is willing to take on all challenges. As it collides with a rock, water produces a beautiful sound. Life is the same. As we go through life, we encounter obstacles, but we're able to advance and grow because of them.

You can't expect not to face obstacles in life. When people meet, their different energies conflict. Where there is no energy, there is no conflict, and where there is no conflict, there is no creation. Conflict is the source of creation. One needs to know how to embrace powerfully the tension that arises when opposing energies meet and there is conflict and struggle.

A peaceful life doesn't mean one that has no conflict or struggle. Just quietly being alone isn't a peaceful life. There are instances where that kind of life is a dead one that's just   pretending to be peaceful. A life that avoids conflict never changes. We must live making sounds like a stream of water—not just small, quiet sounds but big, beautiful ones. We can produce beautiful sounds in our lives by colliding with obstacles.

If we're on the path and we run into something and fall, it's not a shameful thing. It's only a shame if, after we fall, we don't get up again. It's only natural for people to fall, but there are people who, even if they fall, jump back up right away and run forward, and there are people who just keep sitting there, crying. Even when it encounters an obstacle, flowing water always goes on its intended way. If it meets a rock, even if it parts, it goes around and around again and keeps flowing. If there is no path, it makes one.

FAY CANYON

It's an old habit and a hobby of mine to give a name to a tree or rock or place I'm visiting for the first time, depending on the energy that I feel there. Then everything seems a lot friendlier. Thanks to that, even small decorative stones in my home have nicknames.

The first day I went to Fay Canyon, I gave it the name, the "Celestial Canyon." That's how sacred and divinely beautiful it is. There's a spacious, flat, easy forest trail of red sand surrounded on both sides by walls of red rock. It's a comfortable path that makes you feel like you're hiking on a backyard trail, but when you go into the canyon, the view before you makes you feel like you're catching a glimpse of a castle.

If you walk for about twenty minutes from the entrance of Fay Canyon, there's a natural rock bridge to the right. A small sign introduces it at the entrance, but most people pass by without noticing. On a side trail that goes off the main trail, if you follow small piles of stones that act as signposts for about ten minutes, you will reach the bridge. Actually, I didn't know that the bridge was there even on my second visit to Fay Canyon. It was on my third visit that I felt strong energy from that direction, so I went closer and found an arch-shaped bridge.

You can see a stainless blue sky through a crack a few feet wide between the bridge and the rock. Carefully follow the narrow trail on the right and you can even go all the way up to the top of the bridge. There's enough space for about a dozen or so people to sit and do meditation. The rock protruding from the left side of the bridge looks just like the profile of a Native American chief. It's amazing because it's so clear it almost looks like it has been sculpted intentionally.

I often went up on this bridge to meditate. In addition to the fact that it's surrounded by rock on three sides and wide open in the front, the air is exceptionally clear and refreshing. It's hard to imagine Sedona without the sound of birds, but the chirping you hear in this place sounds clearer and deeper than it does anywhere else. From that spot, you can see a rock that I named "Celestial Express." It's shaped like a huge train that came from heaven and is charging this way with its boisterous whistle and billowing smoke.

There are many people who have wondrous spiritual and energetic experiences while meditating on the natural

arch at Fay Canyon. The following is a story shared by one such participant from a meditation tour.

"I was sitting on the natural arch in Fay Canyon, meditating. When I thought of the Celestial Express Rock across the way, it came rushing toward me and then it stopped in front of me. I got on the train with the meditation tour group.

After the train went around several vortexes in Sedona and was boarded by many people, it stopped at Bell Rock, as if that was the final stop. Along with the other people, I got off and went into the light that was pouring on Bell Rock. Inside of that light, people in dazzling white clothes were flying freely and peacefully. I felt like I'd arrived, when I heard this message from deep inside of me: 'Divinity is guiding you in everything you do. Divinity lies within you and manifests in the world through you.'

At the time, I was trying to decide between the work that I really wanted to do and my stable, well-paid job. After my experience at Fay Canyon, I took the risk and dived into the new work. That was the best choice I ever made in my life."

If you come down from the natural stone bridge and hike into the canyon, on the right hand side you will see a rock that looks just like a wine glass. I named that rock "Celestial Glass." If you go farther up for about an hour, you arrive at the end of Fay Canyon. Rocks wrap around three sides like a folding screen, and at sundown they shine with a golden light as they reflect the sun. It's a magical display that lasts for a few minutes, and it's simply amazing.

As a rule, many trees around a mountain make it good for meditation. In this canyon, too, there are many trees emanating a sacred energy. In a canyon like this, I shed the thought that I am looking at the trees and think instead that the trees are seeing me. Focus not only on yourself but also on the trees. When you're talking to another person, if you're filled with your own thoughts, what your counterpart is saying will not even register. The same is true when you're interacting with trees. Empty yourself and feel the trees truly.

If you feel something from the tree, express yourself immediately and with a pure heart. Then the tree will also respond. When you're passing through the forest, there will be a tree that your heart feels drawn to or that you want to touch. Try expressing that feeling exactly as it is. You can place your hand on the trunk and feel the energy of the tree, and you can even have a conversation with the tree. If you meet a good-looking tree, you can say, "You're very good looking," and start up a conversation, as if it were your friend. As you do this, a bond will form between you and the tree, and the tree can even give you a message.

I remember a Mr. Heo who participated in a meditation tour long ago. Due to a disease called cerebral infarction, he had speaking disabilities and partial paralysis of his hands and feet. He had a serious concern. It was smoking. He agonized over his inability to quit even when he knew it was fatal to his health. Even though he had trouble speaking after a single puff, and even though walking became difficult if he smoked a single cigarette, he couldn't bring himself to stop.

When Mr. Heo came to one of my outdoor meditations, he made a big resolution. He thought that this would finally be the time that he quit smoking and, when he was leaving Korea, he tossed his cigarettes and lighter into the trash bin at the airport. But in the end, he couldn't stand it and as soon as he arrived in the US, he bought some cigarettes and had himself a smoke. The first night of the meditation tour, he came to me and, with embarrassment, told me about his dilemma. I asked him to give me his lighter and cigarettes, and in their place, I handed him some fragrant medicinal herbs used by Native Americans.

The next day, we all practiced an exercise in meditation in front of a juniper tree. The exercise involved communicating to the tree whatever you wanted to say, such as questions, thoughts, or feelings that came to you while you were in standing in front of the tree. This gentleman brought up the topic most pressing in his mind, which was smoking. He asked the tree how he could quit smoking. Then he said the tree answered, "It's not that you *can't* quit smoking. It's that you *didn't* quit."

Surprised, he asked, "Why do you think so?"

"It's because you don't have a reason to quit smoking. You have no dream. You don't have something you want desperately to achieve. If you had that, you would treat your body preciously. But because you don't have it, even though you're saying on the outside you're going to quit, in a place deep in your heart, you have this kind of mind: 'I'll just live like this until I die.' Your body has caught on to your mind. That's why you can't quit smoking."

He experienced a big awakening when he heard what the tree had to say, and after that, he was, in fact, finally able to quit.

We say that the red rock mountains of Sedona, the souls of Native Americans, the juniper trees that are hundreds of years old, and the eagle flying through the endless clear blue sky gave us a message, but actually, it's that with the help of Sedona's energy, we have a meeting with ourselves in a state where the various defensive walls surrounding us have come down.

The person who knows you the best is you. We have eyes that watch ourselves. We know what we want. You need courage not to turn away from that. Even when it comes to our own problems, there are many times when we say, "I don't know," and fool ourselves. When we acknowledge that we know something, we have to act on it, so we tell ourselves we don't.

Many people hide inside of their "not-knowing" and, afraid of taking the risk, settle for mediocrity in their life. They imitate the same safe, easy life that other people walk. They mistake that for happiness and, inside of it, look for security. However, the moment that the defensive shields we've built up come down, all truths reveal themselves and speak to us. When we hear our inner voice and follow it, we can walk our own path.

BOYNTON CANYON

Boynton Canyon is the most mysterious and sacred of the four vortexes of Sedona. It is said that the native Yavapai-Apache would not dare enter this area without first purifying their body and mind through fasting or deep meditation. They believed the goddess of this land lived here.

When I go to Boynton Canyon, I always stop at the entrance and offer a prayer. There may be people who think of praying or bowing in front of a mountain as primitive or as a form of idol worship. However, even when you're visiting the home of a close friend, it's courteous to notify them in advance. Even if you're in the same family, when you enter another person's room, you knock. That's the basic etiquette for being considerate of another person. A small mountain embraces innumerable lives. So it's only natural for me to ask if it would be okay to enter. I might say, "I'd like to visit your house today and oblige myself a bit. Please accept me." Giving a greeting like this and politely requesting permission are the right things to do.

Boynton Canyon is a long canyon that would take roughly three hours to hike in and out. I follow the trail that hugs the rocky cliffs across from the Enchantment Resort at the entrance. Low-growing shrubs like agave, yucca, juniper, and so on, line the path, and here and there colorful patches of wildflowers welcome all who come.

After about thirty minutes, the height of the shrubs and trees increases until, finally, you come upon a forest that has grown so tall as to hide the rock cliffs on both sides. The trunks are so thick that even a big person couldn't get his or her arms all the way around them; it's a forest of pine trees and oaks so tall that you have to take a few steps back from the trees to look up and see the sky. Even in the middle of summer, you can feel a chill, and your head clears all the way inside with the fresh, rejuvenating fragrance of the forest.

If you hike comfortably uphill for about an hour, you arrive at the end of Boynton Canyon and a stone cliff that makes a shallow V-shape. At this point, if you follow the path on the right and go up the rock, you can look down on the whole canyon as if you had the eyes of an eagle soaring through the clear blue sky.

This is not a place a lot of people come to at once. It's best for smaller numbers doing deep meditation. I would sit on a rock in Boynton Canyon and practice exercises that involved having conversations with the mountains. In the same way that you can have a conversation with a tree, you can pick a mountaintop that your heart feels drawn to and give energy to and receive energy from it; this is an exchange of heart.

Just as each individual person has their own face, voice, and personality, rocks do, too. Even mountains that all look more or less the same each have their own unique face. Your heart being drawn to a particular mountain means that mountain has energy that resonates with your energy. It means the mountain and you have both accepted and embraced each other.

As you walk through the lush forest of Boynton Canyon, you see a new leaf sprouting from beneath a dying black tree and you see life existing in the shadow of death. You realize that life and death are not separate from each other, but that they coexist. You look around slowly. How much life is embraced by this beautiful canyon and forest?

One day, I got a letter from a working man in his forties who, for three months, had been practicing meditation that I taught in my book. This is what he wrote:

"These days, I wonder if the flowers, trees, clouds, and sky had always been so beautiful, and I'm amazed every day. I never really liked kids. But now, even the face of a child who's throwing a tantrum and crying noisily is so adorable and lovable to me. Now, as I write this letter, a small gnat flies over and sits on this paper. Before, I would have struck it without thinking and gotten rid of it, but now as I look at this tiny creature I think about the source of life . . ."

How did this person become so different? It's because the life inside of him has been awakened. That life rejoices and is glad to see other life. When the life inside of us awakens, we can truly say that "every blooming flower is beautiful." These are not just words. People who feel that, "I really have a bright and beautiful life inside of me," and come to know it, also come to know that other life forms are just like them. That's when we can say that "every blooming flower is beautiful."

When you know that "every blooming flower is beautiful," you realize how wrong it is for one life to dominate another. Although all sorts of trees turn their faces toward the sky to receive the sun, the pine tree doesn't reign over the oak because it's bigger. From the tree that shoots up as though it might pierce the sky to the moss stuck in the crack of a rock, they all live in harmony.

As a rule, all things that have life have a unique color and fragrance. In spite of this, they all get along with each other harmoniously to form a bigger life. A world where they are the same but different and different but the same is a world where every blooming flower is beautiful.

11 THE LAND WHERE PRAYER COMES EFFORTLESSLY

CHAPEL OF THE HOLY CROSS

The Chapel of the Holy Cross belongs to the Roman Catholic Diocese of Phoenix and is a very small chapel in the Saint John Vianney parish. The building was designed by Marguerite Brunswig Staude, a student of the world-renowned ecological architect Frank Lloyd Wright, and was completed in 1956. It is said that one day Ms. Staude was absentmindedly looking up at the Empire State Building at a certain angle when it looked like an enormous cross was hanging on it. That experience inspired her to build this chapel that has a cross covering one entire external wall.

It's obvious that considerable pains were taken to construct a building that is made in harmony with nature without damaging the rock or the surrounding landscape. The chapel

straddles two red rock ridges. The high terrain offers a bird's eye view of Sedona below. Red rocks shaped like people surround the chapel like a folding screen. These rock "people," who look as though they are standing in a circle, have the name "The Twin Nuns." To my eyes, though, those rocks look like the Three Wise Men and the Virgin Mary holding the baby Jesus. If you look out from the chapel, you can see Bell Rock in the distance. It's in just the right spot for receiving its energy.

The Chapel's exterior looks simple, but the inside of the church has a reverent beauty. Perhaps seventy or eighty people could fit inside. The altar couldn't be simpler and the entire wall behind it consists of a window. If you sit in the church praying and lift your head, it seems like the clouds in the sky are racing toward you as though they might be pulled into your eyes. It's a place where prayer comes effortlessly, even if you're just sitting there.

This chapel is close to the house where I lived, so I would pass by on my walks or stop by to meditate and pray. About ten years ago, when I was sitting in the chapel absorbed in meditation, a prayer came to mind. Since at the time I was conducting meditation tours with people from diverse religious backgrounds, what came to me was a prayer of thanks that could be offered with one mind by many people regardless of their religion.

> God who is in heaven
> Thank you for letting us know you.
> God who is in all the mountains and streams
> Thank you for letting us see and feel you.
> God who is in the heart of all people
> I pray earnestly that your will becomes realized.
> What I'm most grateful for
> is that even if I were not to have eyes, ears, and a body
> you have given me this soul
> so that I can know you, who are invisible,
> and for that I thank you with all my heart.

When I come with the meditation tour group, I always make time to stop by the Chapel of the Holy Cross and offer silent prayer. We practice a meditation in which each person offers the most sincere prayer they can, and as they do so, they watch themselves praying. What am I praying for right now? What right now is my sincerest and deepest wish?

The most earnest prayer that I know is to ask for the life energy of the universe to come down into my body and let my mind become full and overflowing with peace and gratitude. Meditation is earnest prayer, and when prayer progresses, it becomes true meditation.

No matter what prayer you offer, or from where, the key to prayer is sincerity. It isn't a certain posture that's important; whatever you do, the important thing is not to lose the feeling of sincere devotion and earnestness. You can kneel if you want to, you can bring your hands together if you want to, and you can bow if you want to.

What I myself guard against is "perfunctory prayer." There are many beautiful prayers composed by other people. I tell people not to recite a prayer written by another person unless it really touches their heart. What matters is your own prayer. You need to offer a prayer that arises from your own sincere heart, the kind of prayer that is so sincere it can move the heart of heaven and earth.

Closing your eyes and bringing your hands together in a reverent position is not the only way to pray. You can pray even while you're working or chatting with someone. I hope you make sure to offer a prayer before you go to sleep and when you start your day. If you make a habit of prayer and meditation, when negative emotions approach you can push them away and take control of them. However, if your connection with the life energy of the universe is broken and you work without prayer or meditation, your life loses its luster and things don't work out well. Work that you squeeze out like you're pressing oil, without peace or joy in your heart, cannot satisfy the soul.

Inside of prayer, we can work creatively. If you become connected with the life energy of the universe through prayer, your head becomes clear as your mind becomes calm and your lower belly becomes warm. As love comes alive in your heart, creativity flows. Also, if your prayer is sincere, action naturally follows. An earnest prayer gives you the strength you need to make plans for what you want and to carry them out proactively.

Feel the energy, starting with your hands, and if you maintain the sensation of being connected to that energy as you pray, you can be more deeply immersed in your prayer. The reason is because the entire universe itself is composed of the energy you're feeling with your hands right now. When you maintain that feeling of connection with the universe as you pray for the great hopes and dreams cherished by your soul, you are broadcasting your prayer to the entire universe as your audience. If the whole universe is resonating with your dream and working with you to make your dream come true, wouldn't that lend great strength to you?

SHAMAN'S CAVE

Shaman's Cave is said to be a place where Native Americans who were chiefs or high priests practiced spiritual rituals. These people would stay here for several days, fasting and receiving validation from the spirits of nature as to whether or not they were qualified to lead their tribe. When the tribe faced great difficulty, such as drought, war, or illness, they would come to this place, burn mystical plants, and sing and dance as they sought answers from Mother Nature.

In Native American society, shamans were unique beings. Not only were they high priests and officiators at ritual ceremonies and ancestral rites who had the ability to converse with the spirits of Mother Nature, they were also political leaders who decided important matters in their tribes. Furthermore, they were like storehouses that preserved the legends of the tribe and other spiritual traditions and, as such, were also responsible for conveying the sacred customs and traditions of the community to the next generation.

This place is not widely known to tourists, so there is not much human traffic here. When I first came here, I felt that the cave refused people. If you come with a group, you may not notice, but there are probably people who would feel afraid if they were to enter the cave alone. I once came below this cave on horseback, but the horse was afraid and suddenly would not go up past a certain point. I had no choice but to tie the horse to a tree below and walk up.

The cave is quite roomy. In the middle of one wall, a hole opens at the height of an adult like a round window, which makes you feel the refinement of Shaman's Cave. Through it you can see a beautiful view of the setting sun and the rising moon. From this cave, there is a good view of the desert and the red rocks of Secret Mountain in the distance. After a short, sweet rain falls on the desert, you can see the rainbow that never fails to hang on Secret Mountain. Below the cliff where the cave is located, there is a small lake where coyotes and javelinas slake their thirst at night.

On the night of a full moon, Shaman's Cave becomes filled with sacred energy. The starlight shining in the jet-black darkness, the moonlight, the howl of the coyote heard in the distance—all are linked by the human breath going in and out. It's a moment in which you sense with your whole being that all life in this world is connected and all life is one.

When I visit this cave, I don't bring a lot of people. That's because the cave has gotten used to quiet stillness over the long years and guards against noise. I come with a small group and we meditate quietly before we leave.

I have sat in this place and done a lot of meditation that involved interacting with the mountains. I gaze quietly at the place where the distant blue sky and Secret Mountain touch. If I focus as I gently open and close my eyes, in the area where the sky and mountain meet I can see ki energy curling and billowing up like heat waves rippling through the air. Along the high and low mountain ridges, I can also see a belt of white-tinted energy embracing the mountain like an aura, and it seems like the mountain is dancing.

I call this place Chunhwa Cave. Chunhwa signifies the ideal death described in the Korean Sundo tradition. It speaks of knowing the reason you were born in this world and, after having lived a life commensurate with that significance, accepting death comfortably and with serenity. The literal translation of the word "Chunhwa" means to become one with heaven. It's the name that I gave after I heard that this cave is where Native American chiefs performed spiritual rituals to prepare for death.

As I sit there and breathe, I think about life and death. Our life and death is no different than the light in a light bulb going on and off. When heaven's ki energy is breathed in through the nose and the earth's ki energy is taken in through the mouth, a connection is made and life "turns on." When our physical life is ended and the soul leaves the body, it's like the light going off. However, just because the light is off doesn't mean that the electricity that powered it has itself disappeared. Life energy itself cannot cease to exist. Death is only the soul leaving the body together with life energy; the life energy itself does not expire.

Innumerable lives come into this world and vanish, but for all eternity, that life does not cease to exist but is absorbed by many other lives and returns to this world. The plants and animals we eat come into our body and our life is sustained. Just as innumerable lives come to us, when our time comes, we ourselves also return to the universe.

It isn't only flowers that wither. It isn't just human life that comes to a close. Even the stars are born and disappear. All of these are aspects of a life that follows the flow of energy of heaven and earth and has a good time playing for a while before going away. People who know this principle do not look at death and shake with fear, but are aware of the greater picture and are able to close their eyes for the last time with joy.

When we are aware that we are eternal beings, when we become enlightened to the fact that our life is something eternal that cannot be harmed by anything, then we have no attachments to the past or anxiety about the future and are able to focus on the present moment—the now.

I make my body and mind neat and clean and sit in this cave, thinking of the Native Americans who accepted the great silence. My mind automatically becomes reverent.

12 SEDONA'S NEIGHBORING VORTEXES

THE GRAND CANYON, Lake Powell, and Rainbow Bridge are not in Sedona. However, they are places that I've visited often; they are places that, to me, were like a seuseung (spiritual guide) who, if I went with a question, would always give me the answers that I sought. I'm introducing these places here because they're ones that many people visit on their way to and from Sedona.

THE GRAND CANYON

How many times have I visited the Grand Canyon? If I think about it, it would easily be more than twenty times. In the early days of the Sedona Meditation Tour, I went several times with my students, and I also stopped by frequently on my way in and out of Sedona; now it feels as familiar as if I were going to a nearby town. It's about a two hour drive from Sedona.

Since the Grand Canyon is the most famous tourist spot in the western United States, the only season in which it's not crowded is winter. For those who prefer quieter places, the fact that there are so many people may be a drawback, but the magnificent energy flooding out of the canyon more than makes up for it. I've come here so often, yet it feels different every time. That's because my mind and energy are different each time I come, but it's also because the Grand Canyon is growing and changing as well.

Just as its name implies, the Grand Canyon is indeed vast and awe-inspiring. Washed and carved by the current of the Colorado River for at least seventeen million years, this massive canyon reaches into the distance and touches the sky. Canyons that are so majestic that you couldn't guess their depth stretch forth in so many layers that you can't see their end. People who are used to living in close quarters are first overwhelmed by its sheer size. I have a vivid memory of when I first visited this place and I marveled at the primeval vital power shooting up from beneath my feet. I was breathing deeply before I knew it. Every time I stand here, I feel the great dignity of this land.

Within the Grand Canyon, there are two Native American reservations. They're located in remote areas that you cannot reach without walking all day or traveling by horse, mule, or helicopter.

There is a legend passed down by the Havasupai Indians. Before humans were born, there were two gods who governed this world. One was a good god and the other was evil. The good god had a beloved daughter named Pukea. He wanted his daughter to go down to the earth and become the mother of creation, to bear life and make it abundant. However, the evil god felt dissatisfied with this plan and caused a great flood to sweep the earth.

The good god cut open a big tree, dug it out, put Pukea inside, and sent her down to the earth. Pukea was swept up by the flood and could only pray for the rain to end as she drifted here and there. At long last, the flood ended and mountaintops and rivers showed themselves. At this time, traces of the raging waters that split the ground as they swept across the plains were revealed, and this is the Grand Canyon.

When Pukea came out of the wooden boat and set food upon the empty earth, a golden sun came up in the East and shone upon the earth. Pukea obtained a son from the sun and a daughter from the waterfall. The son and daughter flourished and, starting with the Havasupai, six Indian tribes were born.

There are several lookouts here that offer magnificent views of the canyon's beauty. Most of the tourists stop by the lookout, make a few exclamations, take pictures, and are already moving on to the next scenic spot. Without giving themselves a chance to feel the immense power poured out by the Grand Canyon, they just briefly allow their eyes some pleasure before they leave.

In order to experience this land properly, you have to step on the red earth as you go down along the winding trail through the canyon. You need to rest in the shade of the pine trees, cool your hot sweat, and look up close at the layers of earth packed together like the thinnest layers of a pastry. Take some deep breaths as you sit beneath the cool energy gushing out from the rocks.

The beauty of the desert comes from its light. The sunrises and sunsets that you see at the Grand Canyon are worthy of being remembered for a lifetime. Watching the sun rise up or go down at the end of the vast land where nothing impedes your view is a fortunate thing. Depending on the direction of the light, the mountains of rock change from moment to moment from scarlet to maroon, and you realize once again how appropriate it is that this place is called "God's masterpiece."

Faced with what Mother Nature created over millions of years, I contemplate how rare it is for a human life to exceed a hundred years and become immersed in thought. This ancient land presents a deep question to human beings. All those things that we've struggled to hold onto with might and main—are they really as significant and precious as we think? What have I lived for?

The Grand Canyon possesses a great purifying power. That's why, if I come here for the meditation tour, we do training that involves sending out stale emotions and taking in the grand energy of the canyon. If, while walking along the trail, a wide flat rock, big shade tree, or a level canyon turns up, we stop walking and everyone sits down and meditates.

It's natural to have emotions or memories that are hard to let go of even when you know they're blocks to your growth. But no matter how deep the hurt or emotion may be, if you let go of it, you *can*. It doesn't even require a lot of time. You can let go of it right away. The problem is that you can't easily separate the emotion or memory from yourself, and there's a part of you that is holding on and trying not to let it go.

There are many who clutch at their sadness as they say, "I'm so sad," or dive deeper into their loneliness as they say, "I'm so lonely." They hold on tight to those emotions and do not let go even while feeling miserable. They can't get over the emotion even though they want to. Whenever I meet people like this, it feels just like a child who has stepped into a puddle of filth and is crying. The puddle isn't that deep and only one foot is in it. All the child has to do is lift his foot out; instead, he just keeps crying for his mother.

The things we are attached to are no more than shadows of the past. However, we do not recognize that, and as long as we hold onto them, they become a part of the present and follow us around. Let's say there's a wound we suffered long ago. The wound closed and left a large or small scar. It's only a scar, and it doesn't interfere at all with your living a healthy life. But to a person who believes the wound is still open, even pain that has since left will return and the closed wound will become infected.

How can we be liberated from negative emotions and

memories? You must first ask yourself with cool objectivity: "Am I really trying to overcome this?" If you can answer "Yes" without hesitation, then you can free yourself from your attachments. The important thing is to be honest with yourself and to have the will and the determination. My emotions are not me; they are mine. My memories are not me; they are mine. I am the master of my emotions and my memories. All you have to do is make up your mind firmly to leave those things behind without attachment or regret and go through with it.

One thing I've learned from teaching many people is that more people than you would expect don't easily follow this simple process. There are many people who are unable to separate themselves from their emotions and see themselves objectively. That's why I teach a meditation in which you purify yourself by visualizing emotions or memories. It's a farewell ceremony of sorts, in which you say goodbye to them. There's no place like the Grand Canyon to practice this meditation. That's because the land itself has already opened people's hearts halfway.

Sit comfortably, close your eyes, and breathe comfortably. Breathe in deeply, and breathe out; as you do so, feel yourself breathing. Imagine there's a bold, intrepid-looking eagle above you. Quietly think of an emotion you want to overcome or a memory that you're ready to release. Hatred, sadness, resentment, envy, jealousy, guilt, self-pity, conceit, memories of being hurt, memories of hurting someone . . . there may be many things that come to mind. Imagine that all those emotions and memories are clumped together into a ball. Call the eagle close to you, and let it take your mass of emotions and memories. The eagle grasps them with its talons and takes flight with deliberate grace. He spreads his large wings majestically and glides slowly through the Grand Canyon sky before drifting down into the canyon to the Colorado River. He flies down into the canyon with power, drops the clump of emotions and memories into the river, and then soars back up into the sky. The strong current of the Colorado River washes over your emotions and memories, which flow down along the river until they gradually dissolve and finally disappear.

After that, fill your body and mind with the majesty of the Grand Canyon. Look at the red rocks, the line of the horizon where the red rocks kiss the sky, look at the clouds, look at the eagle gliding through the sky . . . breathe deeply, and as you fill your lungs, take in this grandeur. The Grand Canyon is grand. But we, as beings with self-awareness, are grander than the Grand Canyon.

LAKE POWELL AND RAINBOW BRIDGE

Even when I'm busy with lectures, writing, and research, there are times when I want to go to Lake Powell. After Sedona, Rainbow Bridge, situated at the end of the lake, is one of my favorite places in the US.

Lake Powell is a man-made lake formed by the Glen

Canyon Dam that crosses the Colorado River, but its scale is so large and beautiful that it doesn't feel artificial. The clear, jade-colored water serenely cuts through 185 miles of desert. After I first visited this place fifteen years ago, I came to so love the many-colored rocks surrounding the lake that glowed golden in the sunset, the reflection of the moon in the lake at night, and the sacred atmosphere exuded by Rainbow Bridge, that I would visit Lake Powell every summer as though I were making a pilgrimage there.

Lake Powell is a haven for water sports and recreation. Because it has all manner of leisure activities such as swimming, fishing, boating, and water skiing, during the summer vacation season it's crowded with people who come with their families to play. However, if you travel by boat to the beach on the opposite shore of the lake, it's quiet and uncrowded. If I come with several students, we put up a canopy on the beach, look at the surface of the lake that sparkles beautifully with sunlight, go swimming, or take a walk on the sandy beach.

The best part of Lake Powell is Rainbow Bridge. If I come with a meditation tour group, we get in a boat right away and head there. The only way to reach Rainbow Bridge is to go in by boat for about two hours or to cut through the Navajo mountains on foot. But in order to hike there, you need to get written permission from the autonomously-governed Native American territory called Navajo Nation.

Rainbow Bridge is the largest natural bridge in the

world. It spans the river like a rainbow as wide as one football field and as high as nine football fields. The Navajo Indians called this bridge the "rainbow that became a rock," and it was a sacred ground. The Navajo mountain where Rainbow Bridge is located figures in their creation myth. The chiefs of the Navajo, Pueblo, and Hopi Indians come to this place and seek wisdom from the spirits of nature, to overcome their shortcomings, and to pray for rain in years of drought.

Until it became widely known in the early 20th century, it was a secret place known only to the local Native Americans and cowboys. After the Glen Canyon Dam was built in 1963 and the level of the river rose, large numbers of tourists began to flock to Rainbow Bridge. In 1974, the local Native Americans became concerned that Rainbow Bridge might become submerged by the lake's rising waters.

To protect their sacred territory, which had been turned into little more than a tourist spot, they initiated a legal battle that, in the end, was lost.

In 1995, however, as a result of an agreement between the National Park managers and Native American tribes, notes requesting that visitors to Rainbow Bridge approach with reverence were posted. Before then, tourists could go right under the bridge. Now, they are asked not to go below the bridge but to look at it from a distance. The Native Americans believed that if one failed to offer a prayer of gratitude prior to crossing under this bridge, great misfortune would occur.

In deep meditation at Rainbow Bridge, several times I saw and felt a Native American saint sitting there. The name of this Native American saint with his long flowing hair was Semu, and standing beside him was a pretty young girl with a band around her head and a bird feather above her left ear. Semu was a superb healer who had the ability to read people's minds and to heal them. There are instances where, in spiritual places like Rainbow Bridge, the visible world and the invisible world come together. Although there may be people who say that such things are nonsense and refuse to believe them, to those who have experienced them it's an undeniable reality. Our visible world is always connected with the invisible one.

Standing before any great sculpture made by nature, anyone would feel reverence, but it's possible to feel that Rainbow Bridge is truly a special place. I received much inspiration here. On my way back from my first visit, lines of poetry came to me and I asked my student who was nearby to jot them down. Here are a few lines of the poem.

> I am here at Rainbow Bridge on Lake Powell
> Where even the sun and moon are not allowed to linger
> Where the pristine beauty of the Earth is preserved
> A place that reveals the earth's intimate layers. . . .

I felt two things when I first stood there. One was grand and beautiful nature, and the other was the heart of the land, the soul of the earth, suffering as if it felt sick.

When I visited with the meditation tour group, we sat and meditated on a wide rock where we could see the bridge. Here, you don't say much. You give two questions for meditation, and after meditating upon that subject by yourself, everyone gets together and tells each other the thoughts and feelings that came to them.

Who am I? And why am I here? Keep asking yourself these questions. Who am I? Who am I? Who am I? Various thoughts and ideas will come up from within your heart. You'll get your own answer, but don't be too easily satisfied by it and keep asking. There is no single correct answer to this question. There is only each individual's enlightenment. What matters is not the answer you give, but how much you focus on the question and how powerfully you collide with it head on.

13 THE FIRST MESSAGE I RECEIVED FROM BELL ROCK

BELL ROCK IS THE ROCK I've climbed the most in Sedona. That first year in Sedona, I would go up to the top several times a day. I would climb up in the morning to watch the sunrise as well as sit in the scorching midday sun. I went innumerable times in the cool sunset, and I also went often in the luminous night of a full moon. I've probably gone to the top of Bell Rock at least a hundred times so far.

Bell Rock is a place of the soul that constantly breathes inspiration into me. Especially when I'm coming up with ideas for something new, such as a new project or new work, I go often to Bell Rock. As soon as I stand at the entrance, it seems like the mountain is welcoming me; when I sit at the top, my mind becomes still as if I've gone up the mountain in my hometown and am looking down affectionately at the

valley below. Even when I'm somewhere else besides Sedona, I usually wake up around three or four in the morning and spend an hour or two in seated meditation. At those times, I also call Bell Rock to mind. That is when creative ideas spring up and problems that I couldn't solve for the longest time are unraveled.

Bell Rock is also the first place I heard the message of Sedona. One day, less than a month after coming, I was meditating at the top, near a small pine tree, and there was a bluebird chirping in the branches.

As I steadied my breath and listened to the bird's song, my meditation became very deep. Though my eyes were closed, I saw an image of butterflies shining with golden light around the pine tree that was next to me. It was beautiful.

When I gave my attention to the butterflies, they flew toward me and started slowly flying in a circle. Every time they fluttered their wings, something like a bright light powder was sprayed out, and then the light started filling the space around me. I'm sure that, since my eyes were closed, what I was seeing was a vision. But it was so vivid that, before I knew it, I was wondering whether it was real or not.

The instant that thought occurred to me, a powerful energy and light poured from the ground where I was sitting, and I felt it shoot through my body, up my spine, through my brain, and out the top of my head. Suddenly, I felt like all of my body's boundaries had disappeared and I had dissolved into light itself.

Inside of that light, I went down into the center of Bell Rock at a high speed as if I were riding an elevator. I suddenly discovered myself sitting in a space filled with all sorts of forms made of different kinds of crystal. I thought, "These crystals are in the shape of the rocks of Sedona." My view was expanded much like when a camera zooms out, and I saw all of downtown Sedona before my eyes.

I was gazing at the rock-shaped crystals as they moved and shone in rainbow colors when a beautiful woman appeared before me. She had long black hair that flowed down to her waist, and deep, dark eyes, though it was difficult to guess her age. Because I had experienced spiritual phenomena like this before during meditation, I was not that surprised, but the sense of the woman's presence was large and impressive.

"Who are you?" I asked.

"I am Sena. I am the goddess who protects Sedona. I have been waiting for you for two thousand years. Welcome to Sedona." She opened her arms wide, and a blindingly bright light radiated from her chest.

"The goddess of Sedona? Then where am I?"

"This is the Crystal Palace, beneath Bell Rock. This is a world that can be entered only through the expansion of consciousness. It's the secret space that connects reality to non-reality," Sena continued. "I am a daughter of Mago, Mother Earth. I invited you here because I have a message that she wants me to deliver to you."

After a brief silence, I heard this message: "Deliver the heart of the earth to humanity."

But rather than being the voice of Sena, it seemed like the entire space was filled with that sound. A bright light poured in through the top of my head, flowed through my chest, and came down to my lower belly. It felt like my body was becoming larger than Bell Rock when, all of a sudden, I exploded. My body became grains of bright light spread throughout the whole space.

A hot energy swirled and wrapped me like a whirlpool; with this sensation I opened my eyes. I was sitting at the top of Bell Rock. Neither the bluebird nor the golden butterflies were there. However, not only was the sensation of hot energy circulating through my body still fresh and real but also the feeling of blindingly bright light powder pouring down was still there. It was difficult to determine what was real and what was an image seen in meditation.

"Deliver the heart of the earth to humanity." The voice was still as fresh as before. It felt as if the entire space was inscribed with the sound of that message and, from there, the same sound was reverberating endlessly.

I knew that this experience was not different from what I had experienced at the moment of enlightenment on Moak Mountain in Korea thirty years before. At that time, the earth came to me and showed me the two futures set out before humanity. This time, the goddess of Sedona, Sena, and Mago's message had come to me.

Bell Rock's Crystal Palace is not an actual physical space that exists beneath Bell Rock. It's another dimension that opened before my eyes when my consciousness expanded and went beyond the world of physical reality. This is something that people cannot perceive through the five senses; instead, it is another reality that exists and can be experienced.

Inside of that space, I felt the deep, deep love of Mother Earth who has never gone to sleep since before we were born and her anguish for the future of the earth and humanity. My heart was filled with this anguish and I felt a sense of mission to deliver Mother Earth's love to all people.

In order not to forget the energy and message of the Crystal Palace, I made a Crystal Room in my house in the room where you can see Bell Rock best. Over the years, I've collected crystals of various sizes, shapes, and colors and filled the space. I even made the ceiling into an octagonal form so that it would harmonize well with the energy of the crystals. This Crystal Room is not for small talk; it is meant only for prayer, meditation, and conversation related to realizing the message that I received during my experience at Bell Rock.

14 THE STORY OF MAGO GARDEN

IT WAS THE SUMMER OF 1996 and it had been about six months since I had come to Sedona. I was busy guiding meditation tour groups that came from Korea twice, sometimes three times a month. Despite my busy schedule, there was something I continued to focus upon. We needed an educational facility where the meditation tour groups that came from so far away could stay comfortably, and where we could develop leaders who could deliver the philosophy and principles of Tao. That's why, for several months, I looked around in the Sedona area for a place that might work well as a meditation center. I kept myself moving and so busy that, even on days when a meditation tour was scheduled, I went out early in the morning or allotted part of my lunch hour to look at places; however, none of them fit the bill.

One morning I was at Bell Rock in deep meditation. When I meditated, it wasn't unusual for me to see apparitions of people who had lived in the region many ages ago, including a myriad of entities in Native American guise. However, this day I was visited by a kindly-looking, elderly white gentleman with a soft smile. He did not say anything, but just gazed at me in a nice way.

Thinking little of it, I closed my eyes again and sank into deep awareness. Then he reappeared and approached me. Feeling that he wanted to speak, I said, "If you have something to say to me, please go ahead." And he replied, "Welcome to Sedona. I am the spirit of a person who came here to teach people and build a community. I died only two years ago."

As soon as he spoke, a whole new scene unfolded in front of me, a moving picture of a wide expanse of striking red earth with small trees and shrubs dotting the landscape. "I have a large area of land in the vicinity of Sedona that I have used as a spiritual training center. I know that the destiny of the land dictates that it become a place of a new spiritual awakening. I also know that the ultimate realization of this destiny is not with me, but with you. Please take this land and use it in accordance with its destiny." The apparition faded quickly as the moving picture of the land dissolved into a brief glimpse of various people; then that, too, disappeared.

After coming down from Bell Rock, I resolved to find out if what the old man had said was true, and I headed to Sedona's top realtor. I gave him a rough description of the land that I had seen in meditation and asked if he knew of a retreat center in the Sedona area.

He replied that he certainly knew of such a place and that he was the real estate agent of record for that particular piece of property! We set out immediately and drove for about forty minutes from the center of Sedona, along an unpaved road, until we came to about 160 acres that lay nestled in the middle of a national forest preserve. Rows of small casitas, half hidden by the red earth, blended in harmoniously with the land. The agent explained that all of the retreat's buildings had been designed to be "nature-friendly." From every angle, red rocks piercing the blue sky formed a stunning background. Below, the land was a desert forest of juniper trees and cactus plants.

I was given a tour not only of the land but also of the dilapidated, but curiously appealing housing units for visitors

and guests. The guide asked me whether I knew about the founder of this retreat center and handed me a book that the man had written. I was shocked, for as soon as I glanced at the book, I recognized the author's face with the same expression and gentle smile he had shown me at Bell Rock. I asked the guide to tell me the story of the man and the retreat center in more detail.

The founder's name was Lester Levenson. He had died in 1994, on the very land on which we were standing. He was originally from New York, a physicist by training, and a successful businessman. However, in 1952, at the age of forty-two, he'd had the second of two heart attacks. Although he survived, his doctor sent him home, telling him that there was nothing that the hospital could do for him. It was a death sentence. He had only a few months to live.

Filled with anger and despair, Levenson was forced to examine every single moment of his life. He contemplated suicide. However, as his death's inevitability slowly faded from his mind, he realized that he was still breathing and still a thinking being with nothing to lose. So he decided to try an experiment with his body, emotions, and consciousness. As he sat quietly in his home, deeper questions about life arose, commanding his attention.

"What is life?" "What am I looking for?" The first answer that rose to his mind was "happiness." He then asked himself, "When did I feel most happy?" The answer that first came to him was "When I received love," but he knew that was untrue. Although he had had many lovers, friends, and family members who loved him, he was not always happy. So he examined all the moments of genuine happiness in his life. He finally concluded that he felt genuinely happy only when he had given love to others.

He then asked, "If the moments of unhappiness in my life were the result of my heart not being filled with the giving spirit of love, then might I not turn back the clock in my mind and fill those moments with love, transforming them into happiness?" If happiness was an emotion generated by his state of mind, then, he surmised, he could indeed transform the unhappy moments in his life into happy ones.

He immediately recalled his most recent unhappy experience. It was when he was told by his doctor to go home to wait for death. Though he had previously felt rage at the doctor for forcing him to go home, thinking that perhaps the doctor did not want a patient to die while in his care, Levenson now thought about how very difficult it must have been for the doctor to tell him that he was going to die. The important thing now was whether he could transform the anger that he had felt for the doctor into love. He tried his best to recall those moments of rage and despair and melt them away until eventually he succeeded in replacing his anger with love. He realized, at that exact moment, he was indeed happy.

His experiment continued. For three months—the amount of time he had been allotted to live—he sat in his home and brought up every single face, every possible moment of his life, one by one, to release any associated negative emotions.

As he pursued his efforts, his heart overflowed with love and joy.

The most difficult thing to do was to face the fear of his own death. By realizing that the fear of death lay at the root of all negative emotions, he was able to open his heart wide and burn away his fear of death with the flame of his newly recovered love. By letting go of every mundane attachment, Levenson was able to let go of his attachment even to life.

Once his fear of death was gone, his body felt as light as a feather, and he was certain that the disease had left him. Three months after the doctor's gloomy prognosis, he felt an indescribable joy that soon led him into a world of quiet inner peace. In this world, which alternately soothed and energized him, he realized that his current physical manifestation as "Lester Levenson" was not his deepest and truest identity . . . he was not his body or his thoughts. He was something far deeper that went to the source of all life, a "beingness" that was eternal.

Wanting to share what he had learned, he spoke at seminars and to small, spiritually-minded groups of people. Soon people flocked to hear his amazing and inspirational story, and his audience swelled to several hundred people.

In 1958, he felt a sudden urge to head west. On his way to San Diego, he passed through Arizona and spotted a sign that read "Sedona." He heard an inner voice tell him, "Go there!" Guided by this voice, he went immediately to Sedona and was overwhelmed by the unique combination of breathtaking beauty and spiritual energy. He decided to purchase a farm in a remote area for a meditation and retreat center. Here he told people of his experiences and shared the methods by which they, too, might experience the same realization. These techniques eventually became known as the Sedona Method.

The Sedona Method became famous worldwide, with thousands of people practicing it. His closest students in New York visited him often in Sedona, with some of them moving to be near him. He continued to share his insights with all who were drawn to his presence. Lester Levenson, who was told he would die at the age of forty-two, lived until he was eighty-four and was active until the end of his life.

Such was the grand story of the land I was looking at for the first time in the searing heat of that summer day. I was deeply impressed by Lester Levenson's story and felt a close kinship with him. His suffering and fear and his awakening and enlightenment seemed like they were my own. I was, however, most surprised to hear from the center's staff what he had said just before he died: "Soon an awakened soul from the East will come to use this land to awaken many other souls. I am simply the person who is preparing this land for his arrival."

Because controversy had surrounded ownership of the land, even while Levenson was alive, he had not willed it to anyone, not even to his closest students. When I first went there, it had been two years since his passing, and the ownership issue was headed to the courts with several claims to the land by his numerous students.

As I looked at the land from a hilltop, I recalled what Levenson's soul had said to me. He had said that he wanted me to use the land for my purposes. No matter how "right" his message felt, however, there was no way this could realistically happen.

"It's all well and good to tell me to use this land, but it's another thing for me to actually attempt to buy it. We simply do not have the financial wherewithal to afford this . . . and what if we did acquire it? It's a huge piece of land in the middle of the Arizona desert. Even Americans failed to run this place in the black . . . what can we inexperienced Koreans do? We don't have any business foundation in America, and we don't even speak very good English."

Such were my thoughts, a combination of hope, doubt, and wry humor, as I considered the message I had received from the gentleman on Bell Rock. Then I thought, "Although I know that Lester Levenson is a sincere soul, how can I be sure that his message is true? I wish that he had been more specific about the land and its possibility for future use . . . a map to a nearby buried treasure wouldn't hurt, either."

On that day, I had no choice but to turn back, and I decided to forget about the land. However, whenever I meditated, Levenson's soul would come to me and gaze at me in silence with a certain longing before it disappeared. When I told him that it was not possible for me to take over his center, he would just circle around and gaze at me with a pensive look.

Soon he started to appear in my dreams, and I decided to go back once more to see the land where a thriving retreat center had once stood. Lost in my thoughts and the land's mesmerizing beauty, I took a long, leisurely walk along its many trails. I encountered a small and neglected grave, seemingly lost among the wild desert grasses. The headstone indicated that here lay Lester Levenson. In a moment of piercing empathy, I felt the sweat and tears that he must have shed to create and fulfill his vision on this patch of Earth. I felt the overflowing love, the weariness, and the loneliness.

I was forced to reconsider my previous decision. Should I risk everything I had achieved over the past fifteen years in order to obtain a single, large piece of land in the middle of a beautiful but foreboding desert because of the entreaties of one departed soul? All of my closest colleagues and students tried to dissuade me. In the following months, I visited the land several more times, always plagued by the nagging and momentous question of "Should I or shouldn't I?"

Then, one day, I read in the local newspaper that the land of the late Lester Levenson would be put up for public auction to pay off the legal fees that had accrued as a result of the long legal battle among his students over its ownership. Now I was out of time. I had to buy the land or let it go forever. I decided to visit one last time before making a final decision.

As was the case with each previous visit, I was overwhelmed by the surrounding scenery and powerful energy of the land, yet saddened by the state of disrepair and neglect of the retreat center. As I once again walked up to Levenson's grave site, the tall, unkempt sea of wild grass greeted me with an undulating sway. A fierce wind blew and kicked the red dry dirt up in a swirl; it was almost as if the land itself was crying out for love and hope of a new incarnation. I stopped as I felt the heart of the land beating to the rhythm of its own sadness. Suddenly, a powerful tremor rumbled underneath my feet, accompanied by an inner voice that cried out resoundingly, "Will you truly forsake me?"

A jolt of electricity went through me as every cell in my body responded to the call of the land with a cry equal in power and longing. "Is this what you truly want of me?" Just then, incredibly, a bolt of lightning struck only a few feet from where I was standing, crackling loudly as dry dirt spewed violently into the air. Shaken by the experience, I fell to my knees in humble submission. "I shall do what you ask . . ."

Yet no matter how truthful or powerful a message is, one is nevertheless confronted with fear for the future when the path that's shown appears to lead to certain ruin. But when the message comes from the source of life, then you have no choice but to accept it, however impossible it may seem at the time. There was no other option.

After many logistical and legal complications, the purchase of the land was finally made possible through the generous support of Tao Fellowship, a nonprofit organization whose mission is to further the cause of peace worldwide by promoting the spirit of Tao. Thus, Sedona Mago Garden was born after many months of labor pains.

Mago means *Mother Earth* in Korean. Sedona Mago Garden is the nickname for the Sedona Mago Retreat Center. The center runs programs for spiritual awakening and holistic learning for individuals and groups from all walks of life. People come to participate in the spiritual practices and ceremonies and refresh their whole being in Sedona Mago Garden's beautiful, awe-inspiring natural settings.

When we bought this land, neither I nor any of the executive staff of Tao Fellowship had done any prior business calculations. When I made the decision to buy it, I didn't consult with professionals. Because we didn't have a business plan, it was all too obvious what kind of conversation, if we'd had one, would have transpired between us and the professional consultants.

"Do you have any experience with regard to acquiring and operating a place like this?"

"No."

"Do you have enough money to run this place?"

"No."

"Do you have competent staff who can work here?"

"No."

"Our conclusion is simple. You absolutely should not buy this place. Unless you want to go under."

Then this is what I would have said to them: "We have a dream. And a message that this land gave us."

And then they would have shaken their heads, unable to understand.

All we had was our dream and our will. No, there was another thing; that would be our supporters, to whom we are truly grateful, who participated so actively in that dream. These people came to share our dream through the Sedona Meditation Tour, they made donations when we were buying Mago Garden, and they helped us with all their material and emotional support as they volunteered their time or their professional expertise and experience. That's how all the sincere devotion of many people was gathered, bit by bit, and the energy of this land called Sedona Mago Garden slowly started to come to life.

15 THE LAND WHERE THE HEART OF THE EARTH CAN BE FELT

THE CHALLENGES THAT had to be overcome after Mago Garden was acquired were bigger than even I had expected. Just repairing and cleaning the buildings that hadn't been cared for in years took a lot of time. Like pouring water in a bottomless jar, endless investment and effort was required.

Running the place was a bigger issue. Fortunately, as Tao members from Korea and the US participated regularly in Mago Garden's meditation and Tao programs, we were able, little by little, to overcome these difficulties of operations. Through the patience and selfless effort of the Mago Garden staff and the generous love and support of Tao members from the whole world, we got through the most difficult period, and Mago Garden started to become established.

Early on a summer day in 2001, I went up a nearby hill from which I had a bird's-eye view of Mago Garden. I was looking out at the juniper tree forest and fields in the distance. I took a deep breath and the fresh morning air filled my chest. The desert was waking up as the morning sun had just begun to rise. All sorts of birds—quail, swallows, sparrows, towhees—were chirping, calling out their morning greetings to each other, and even the dry leaves and cactus needles were twinkling in the morning light. The desert that had been so still was becoming active as it started a new day.

I took my time and gazed for a long time at Mago Garden, which was growing more visible in the morning sunlight. I looked very carefully at each and every building, each and every tree, and even each and every trail, one by one. Thanks to the sincere devotion poured into it by many people over the past four years, Mago Garden, which had been so lonely and abandoned, was now starting to be filled with energy. I drew a picture in my mind of how Mago Garden could change in ten years.

The multi-colored flowers that blended with field plants, the flourishing trees that provided shade from the midday sun, the lake where birds and wildlife quenched their thirst, the cozy and endearing trails made me think: *like me, many people will look at the morning desert from this spot and receive inspiration, hope, and courage.*

I imagined people from all parts of the world with different faces, colors, languages, and religions coming here and studying the Tao, praying and meditating together, opening their hearts, and becoming one; and I imagined each of these people returning to their lives to live the Tao and cultivate themselves and the lives around them so beautifully. My heart became full as deep emotion and gratitude swept over me.

I came down from the hill and went to Lester Levenson's grave. Now he felt comfortable and dear, like a friend with whom I'd spent a lifetime and who had passed away before me.

"I know you asked me to take this land and awaken the souls of many people . . . it's already been four years. I've been working really hard to keep my promise to you and to heaven. What do you think? Do you like it?"

Lester Levenson seemed to be nodding as he smiled his characteristically gentle smile. There was still a long way to go, but even so, I felt a sense of relief and satisfaction that at least the first few difficult steps had been successfully taken. I made my resolution once again. *We'll really make Mago Garden into a place that awakens many people's souls; we'll make everyone who comes here feel the heart of the earth.*

When repair of the internal facilities was completed, we started pouring our devotion into cultivating the exterior and landscape of Mago Garden. We planted flowers like oleander, yucca, pampas grass, daffodils, and sunflowers, which would grow well even in the harsh desert sun, as well as cacti, which were decorated with blossoms in brilliant white, yellow, and intense pink in summer. Every so often I would go to Flagstaff and buy flower seedlings and make flower beds at the entrance of Mago Garden.

On the weekends, the Tao members in Sedona and Phoenix would come to Mago Garden and we would tend the land together. Tao program participants would come from Los Angeles, New York, Chicago, Houston, and other places, and stay a few extra days to help plant flowers and trees. They were not reluctant to face the broiling heat of the Arizona desert and picked up hoes and shovels to plant cottonwood trees and cart rocks for flower beds. At night, we gathered together to meditate in the starlight and moonlight of Sedona.

At dusk, Secret Mountain off in the distance would reflect the setting sun and shine with a golden light that warmly embraced Mago Garden. The Sedona night sky that you look up and see here is something that no one could forget. Every time the large, thick stars twinkle, it's like the heart of the sky is beating. When the full moon rises above the dark silhouette of Secret Mountain, Mago Garden's trees and even the ripples of its lake answer the moonlight with a beautiful dance and song of life.

"People's hearts color the heart of the earth and the heart of the earth colors the hearts of people." I said this often to those who volunteered at Mago Garden and to whom I was so grateful. I would also tell them, "This land will remember the love and devotion we poured into it today. If the hearts of the people who are living and breathing and eating together here at Mago Garden, and the hearts of the people who come here to study and share the Tao are beautiful and holy, then this land will also become beautiful and holy. Furthermore, through the help of this sacred land, even more people will discover their greatness within."

The place that we cultivated with the sincerest devotion was the Healing Garden. I wanted the people who visited Mago Garden to feel Nature's healing energy to their heart's content. Healing energy emanates from the powerful sun and red earth, but if water energy and wood energy were added, it's even better. That's why we envisioned a Healing Garden with a lake and abundant flowers and trees.

In the southwest of Mago Garden, there was a reservoir where the land was low. Because it had not been properly cared for over a long time, it was filled with mud and aquatic weeds and almost unable to function as a reservoir. We restored the reservoir to its original condition. When the rainy season came, the rain collected there and the lake took shape. Around the lake, we made a trail and planted flowers.

We put our plans into action one by one. We started with our plan to create a lake. In the beginning, gathering water in the lake was a big challenge. Eventually, we had enough water in the lake, but there were too many aquatic weeds. To prevent the aquatic weeds from taking over, we installed an underwater pump that circulated the water and even built a fountain in the center of the lake. We constructed a waterfall and a small island that you could reach via a small bridge, where we planted a graceful willow tree. Then we cut and smoothed two parallel trails so people could walk easily around the lake, one of coarse gravel and one of fine gravel. We bred koi in the lake and planted lotuses as well.

Here and there along the banks of the lake, we made special meditation and resting spots, which were landscaped with flowers, trees, and herbs that emanate subtle scents. There had been nothing at all on this piece of land when we started, but we never gave up, and the growth continues to this day. The Healing Garden, for example, is continuously evolving through the process of creating something from nothing.

With the completion of the lake, the nearby wildlife naturally started to come to drink, so it became possible to see deer and wild peccaries (javelinas) there with their noses gently touching the water. And, of course, there are many wild birds, bees, and butterflies. A mated pair of great blue herons comes during the winter season to enjoy the bounty of the lake. Sometimes you can see them flying gracefully through the blue Sedona sky with their beautiful outstretched wings. Every so often, on murky days that threaten rain, you can even see moles busily digging the earth. The Healing Garden is an amazing place that embraces not only people, but also every living creature around Mago Garden.

Another one of our longtime hopes was to build an educational facility at Mago Garden that could accommodate many people. At the time that the property was purchased, the large hall was the space currently being used as the dining hall. That space can only accommodate about fifty people, and because the kitchen and hall are adjacent to each other, we found during the training sessions that the aroma of food was an extraordinary interference. On one side of the wall, people were insanely busy preparing food and, on the other, people were practicing prayer and meditation.

The construction of a new educational facility that could accommodate two hundred people was begun in 2001. The day we broke ground, heaven gave us a gift of dazzlingly clear twin rainbows that tied together the southern and northern ends of Mago Garden. That is how the current Mago Chapel was constructed, and several years afterward, eighty more guest rooms were added.

We tried to uphold a high standard of eco-friendliness when we developed Mago Garden. Our score on the Northern Arizona Green Checklist developed by the Coconino Sustainable Economic Development Initiative was Five Leaves, the highest level of the rating system.

In one part of Mago Garden, we went through years of

trial and error cultivating an organic farm. Now, fresh vegetables and fruit grown at the farm are offered on the Mago Garden menu, and quite a few people come from nearby to hear the success story of our organic farm.

In the organic garden, we grow various vegetables such as lettuce, peppers, squash, green onions, and tomatoes; herbs such as basil, rosemary, and sage; and fruit such as apples, grapes, melons, and peaches. In the spring, white pear blossoms and pink cherry blossoms are in bloom, with bees buzzing about. In the fall, delectable jujubes hang from every branch, and we share them with our neighbors and the visitors to Mago Garden. When the fruit ripens, its sweet fragrance is carried by the breeze. We've also raised about thirty chickens, some of whom in the beginning were victims of coyotes and eagles, but now they're all healthy and well.

The time I feel the most rewarded is when I see Tao members who come here reach a significant turning point in their lives through a profound experience of coming face to face with themselves. Every time I see that, I feel a sense of gratitude and it's as if all the years of struggle and hardship are washed away in an instant. And I feel deep gratitude, too, toward all the people, starting with Lester Levenson, who helped us to realize that dream.

16 CONNECTIONS CREATED BY SEDONA

I'VE MET A TRULY LARGE number of people in America. From restaurant chefs to meditation guides, truck drivers, scholars, media personalities, writers, meditators, religious leaders, peace activists, and those who are said to be difficult to meet, including movie actors, celebrities, sports stars, a professional baseball team owner, and politicians, I've met all kinds of people from all walks of life.

Although many encounters were accidental, many more of these meetings I had to "create." None of them had been waiting to meet me. These notable people, in particular, were not the sort you could meet easily just because you wanted to meet them. I had a sense of urgency, a feeling that I had to meet people who could understand and share my dream, for I had a dream. That urgency pushed me to create those connections. And most of those connections began with something very small.

The work of creating those connections started in a little restaurant called "Manzanita" in Sedona. The food was great. I gave the chef my heartfelt thanks for a delicious meal. We talked for a while and I discovered that he was the owner of the restaurant and a former head chef on the famous cruise ship, the Queen Elizabeth. A look at his face gave me the impression that he had a health problem, so I taught him a few simple training methods I thought would help. After training by himself for a few days and experiencing its effectiveness, Al, the restaurant owner, told me that he would like to take private lessons from me twice a week. In this way, he became my very first member in Sedona.

During my early days in Sedona, there were, evidently, quite a lot of rumors about me circulating among the real estate agents whom I had met as I had searched so passionately for land on which to establish a meditation center. One day, having heard the rumors, a man who called himself a "walking Sedona encyclopedia and map" came to see me. I realized at our first meeting that what he said included a lot of hot air, but if there was anything to learn from him about Sedona, even something very small, I wanted to learn it. I was talking with him once when he happened to mention that a woman named Hanne Strong was supporting meditation groups and spiritual organizations in Colorado; I drove fifteen hours to see her.

Hanne Strong didn't find me very interesting. Our first meeting ended in the exchange of a few words that were just a formality. A few months later, Ms. Strong was scheduled to visit Korea with her husband when I was in Korea, and I ended up meeting her in Seoul. I heard the news then that Hanne was going to the enthronement ceremony of a reincarnated Nepali lama, and I decided to go with her. I made up my mind to take part in the trip, but it was not because I had time in my schedule or because I was interested in the ceremony to be held in Nepal.

I took part in that trip because my encounter with Hanne Strong was meaningful, and because of my intuition that I had something to create with her. I was able to talk a lot with Hanne over the course of several days. Her attitude toward me changed a great deal after that trip. We became friends who understood each other and supported each other's activities.

After that, many links with other people were forged through her. I came to be good friends with Maurice Strong, her husband, who was once Under-Secretary-General of the United Nations.

I also met Professor Seymour Topping. This giant of journalism, who once served as Editor-in-Chief of the *New York Times* and Chairman of the Pulitzer Prize Committee, introduced many global leaders to me. These individuals participated or cooperated in the founding and organization of the New Millennium Peace Foundation, a nonprofit

organization. They came all the way to Korea to take part in the "Humanity Conference: Earth Human Declaration," of which I was conference chairman.

There is another connection created for me by Sedona. About two years after purchasing Mago Garden, I was in the midst of planning a program called "Meeting with the Creator," in which Korean and American Tao Members would both participate. It was then that I got some good news. Neale Donald Walsch, author of the bestseller *Conversations with God*, would be coming to Mago Garden to hold a group workshop for his readers. I invited him to give a lecture at Meeting with the Creator, and I also gave a lecture to his group.

At the time, we had no lecture hall able to accommodate several hundred people, so I created one by pitching a huge white tent on a hill overlooking the golden sunsets of Secret Mountain. As we talked, Neale and I understood each other right away. I spoke with him a great deal because he was the first person I had met in the United States with whom I shared such a mutual understanding. My time of searching and my experience of enlightenment in Korea, my dreams, and my sense of mission, what I felt about the human race and the Earth all prompted Neale to advise me seriously, "The world has got to hear your story and message. Publish a book." He also actively helped me by introducing me to a publisher and providing me with feedback on my manuscript.

In that way, my first book in English, *Healing Society*, was published in 2000. The book served as a bridge for me to formally introduce to American society my philosophy, Dahn Yoga, and Brain Education. Afterward, thanks to the efforts of my students, hundreds of Dahn Yoga centers appeared in America, Japan, Canada, and several countries in Europe.

All of these are a result of precious connections created for me by Sedona and Mago Garden. Had I passed by Sedona fifteen years ago or had a realistic calculation of potential losses kept me from acquiring Mago Garden or had Tao members and friends like Neale Donald Walsch not come to this place, we would never have seen such results.

I believe these connections are not the result of chance. They are the result of long cherished hopes, choices, and creation. I considered precious even very small connections, and when I cultivated and developed them, they led me to other connections.

Whether I met the chef of a small restaurant or a famous political leader, I would talk about my dream to them all in the same way. Even in the case of those who at first treated me with disinterest, through certain opportunities that disinterest would eventually change into curiosity, and after a while, once they sensed my genuineness, they would turn into partners who were generous in their active support.

All connections, when viewed indifferently, are nothing more than passing fancies. All connections—great and small—that come to those who have a dream, and stay focused on that dream, change into gifts for realizing their dreams.

17 MAGO CASTLE COMES TO US

IT HAPPENED AT A TIME when I was spending a lot of time climbing Bell Rock after first settling in Sedona. One night the moon was very bright. Showing their silhouettes under the moonlight, the rocks of Sedona were truly beautiful and mysterious. All around me the world was quiet. Still as a night at sea, the whole universe was asleep, and it seemed that only the moon and stars and I were awake. From Bell Rock I was looking toward West Sedona, and there was one point that caught my eye.

A peak stood close to West Sedona. Bright light shone upward from its summit. It was located at the center of three of Sedona's four great vortexes—Bell Rock where I was seated, Cathedral Rock across the way, and Airport Mesa. Energy from those three vortexes was flowing into this one place.

The next day I went to where I thought the place might be to confirm it for myself. It was clearly the summit of the hill that rises midway between Cathedral Rock and the Chapel of the Holy Cross. The winding road that goes up to the peak was lined by houses on both sides. When I arrived at the point where there were no more driveways, I got out of the car and looked around. There was a house with its front gate closed; hanging on it was a sign that read, "No Trespassing." It looked like a privately owned home. The sign kept me from entering the place. I had no choice but to wait until someone came out.

I wanted to go into the house and feel the energy. This was no ordinary place if the energy I had seen the night before was from here. The scenery in front of the house was amazing enough, but I was very curious about what the view would be like from the house's courtyard.

I waited and walked back and forth for maybe thirty minutes. That's when I saw a young woman come out. Full of expectation and glad to meet her, I greeted her first in a loud voice.

"The energy of this place looks so wonderful. I'm sorry, but would you mind if I took a look around the house for just five minutes?"

My polite request was immediately rejected. The young woman went into the house and closed the gate behind her.

An Asian she had never seen before says he'd like to come in and look around a house that has not even been put on the market. It's no surprise that the woman refused. Even so, being refused like that, I honestly felt ashamed and disappointed. I had waited for a long time, and the thought of just having to go back down the hill stopped my feet from moving. I approached the front gate again only to retreat, and after repeating this a few times and having no other choice, I gave up and turned around to go on my way.

I was walking toward my car when I saw Bell Rock to my right, off in the distance. I mumbled to myself, as if I were making a promise to Bell Rock: "It looks like I'll have to become this house's owner if I'm going to properly experience the energy of this place. Within ten years, I'm going to look on you, Bell Rock, from the courtyard of this house without regret."

I almost never thought of this promise after that. Maybe I forgot about it. I was really busy those first few years. After taking over Mago Garden, along with my students, I poured all of my attention into revamping that place and educating them through the Tao programs.

After eight years had passed, one day a real estate agent told me that the house in question was up for sale. On hearing the news, my heart pounded and I wanted to rush right over to see it. I guess it had been sitting there somewhere very deep in my consciousness.

When I visited the house, I met an elderly woman in her early eighties. She told me this story:

The woman's husband had been a psychology professor at UCLA. Long ago, they had made a trip to Sedona and, by accident, had come upon this hilltop. There was a rundown old house on top of it at the time. Enthralled by the amazing

scenery, her husband wanted to build a beautiful house there where they could spend their retirement. The owner of the lot, however, said that he'd die before he'd sell.

They never gave up, however, and ended up buying the land after waiting more than a decade. The couple then moved to Sedona. At the time they bought the land, the husband was almost eighty and in poor health. Following two years of laborious work, construction of the house was completed, and the husband lived there for six months before passing away.

After her husband died, the elderly woman was herself close to eighty, so it was more than a little uncomfortable for her to drive up and down that steep road. And the big house was in such a high spot that, when the weather was rough, it would echo with the rushing sounds of wind and rain.

The woman ended up putting the house on the market, and many people showed interest in it, as it was famous for its scenic beauty. A Hollywood couple even put money down on it, but then cancelled their purchase when they suddenly decided to divorce. For several years, many people showed interest, she said, but the sale would never go through because, strangely, something unexpected would always come up.

When I visited the house, I was able to guess why such things were happening. The energy of the place was truly special. You could say that it was not of this world. Standing there, it was like my body had been lifted off the ground into the heavens. I could feel my head emptying and a clear energy pouring down into me through the crown of my head.

My field of vision was unrestricted in every direction. From the front yard, Bell Rock is visible and Cathedral Rock stands right before your eyes. Cathedral Rock is well known for showing different aspects of itself, depending on the angle from which you view it. From that vantage point, the front of the rock looked like the profile of a person with hands clasped in earnest prayer.

The feeling I got there, in short, was that here was "a place that touches heaven." Here you could feel the majesty of the Earth, as if it is the place that chooses the man, not the man who chooses the place.

When I had stood in front of that house eight years

before, I had said I would eventually become owner of this land, but I hadn't really thought about what that meant. After actually visiting the place, though, my thinking changed. It's not the kind of land that an individual can own. It's too special to be the possession of one individual or family. I came to feel that the land must be used by many people and for some lofty purpose.

I proposed that the nonprofit Tao Fellowship buy the land and use it as a space of prayer and meditation. However, I found myself confronting the same situation I'd faced when we acquired Mago Garden: Tao Fellowship, which had only just begun operating, did not have enough funds. The other executives of Tao Fellowship and I again started thinking earnestly about a solution.

Although funding was one problem, I also felt oppressed by an incredible sense of responsibility. This is because I felt we must not buy the land unless our intentions were pure, unless we intended to use it solely for the human race and the Earth, and unless there were no other ulterior motives. But why were we seeking to invest so much money in buying this land? Were we really ready to use it for a holy purpose? There were questions I asked myself as I stood in the front yard of the house, looking at Bell Rock.

Meanwhile, the elderly woman wanted to sell the house as quickly as possible. She seemed ready to sell it to someone else unless I made a decision right away. We might never get another chance to buy the land if we missed this opportunity. The directors of Tao Fellowship and I thought long and hard about it, and then offered her the best price we could. However, it fell far short of what she wanted.

The woman fretted over our offer as the real estate agents worked hard to close the sale. Thankfully, she eventually accepted after coming to understand the purpose of the nonprofit Tao Fellowship. That's how this special land became the property of Tao Fellowship. I named it "Mago Castle," meaning it was a place where we could receive the messages of Mother Earth.

This is a residential area, and the lot has many neighbors, so it's not the kind of place that many people can visit all at once or one that we can keep open all the time. Here at Mago Castle, once a month we offer a ritual sacrifice to heaven in which we pray for humanity and the earth. And, in very special cases, a small group of Tao members come here to hold prayer and meditation ceremonies. Before praying at Mago Castle, they purify body and mind through several days, or several months, of practice.

This place, Mago Castle, is truly blessed ground. In the morning, brilliant sunshine pours down on its little backyard where violet herbal flowers are in full bloom. Standing in that light, you feel as if your body is melting into the sunshine and becoming light itself. In the dazzling sunlight, the Chapel of the Holy Cross, and the rocks surrounding it, one or two at a time reveal their true forms.

The form of Cathedral Rock spreading out before Mago Castle is truly a magnificent sight that changes constantly according to the angle of the light striking it. About the time

that the sun in the west paints the crimson rocks an even deeper shade of red, the moon gradually rises in the east. The full moon raises its head, casting its subtly golden rays of light over the rocky mountains to the east. The beautiful silhouettes of Bell Rock and Cathedral Rock come alive under the full moon. If you then look toward where sky and ground touch, you'll feel a shiver run through your body, moved as you are by the sacredness of that time and space.

On nights without a full moon, starlight fills the heavens above Mago Castle. Scattered across a sky as dark as black mud are clumps of stars that it seems you could touch if you would but stretch out your hand. The moonsets are even more deeply moving than the sunsets. The setting of a full, round moon in particular creates a beautiful glow in the sky. Even before the reverberations of the moonset fade from your mind, the sun is already preparing yet another cosmic show in the east. From Mago Castle you can witness a vibrant cosmic show four times a day: when the moon rises in the east, following the setting of the sun in the west and when the sun rises out of the east, chasing the sinking moon in the west.

I don't use the expression, "We bought Mago Castle." I say that Mago Castle came to us. Anyone standing here at Mago Castle feels deeply moved by the grandeur of life and comes to ask the holy question, "What should I do with this life?"

18 WHAT MAGO MEANS TO ME

THE REASON I'VE GIVEN the name "Mago" to Mago Garden, Mago Castle, and many other places in Sedona is because the first message I received here was: "Share the heart of the Earth with humanity." Meaning "mother earth" and "earth spirit," Mago is a name that appears in the book, *Budoji*, written around 400 CE by Jesang Park, a famous scholar during the Shilla Dynasty in ancient Korea. In the Western tradition, this same concept is commonly known as "Gaia."

Every ethnic group has myths and tales depicting their ideals. In all times and places, such stories tell us what it is that we genuinely and unchangingly pursue.

The *Budoji* begins like this:

"In the beginning, Yullyeo was reborn several times and the stars appeared; Mago and Mago Castle emerged from Yullyeo."

Yullyeo is the fundamental rhythm of life that created the universe. Yullyeo is filled with the three elements that penetrate all life—light, sound, and vibration.

The story continues: A perfect being having both male and female natures, Mago alone gave birth to two daughters, and her two daughters alone gave birth to two sons and two daughters each. These four pairs of males and females were divided into Yellow, White, Black, and Blue tribes, and lived within Yullyeo on the clear milk of the Earth, which wet the ground like dew.

Then, again through the rhythm of Yullyeo, Mago made the land and sea appear on the Earth. Air, fire, earth, and water mixed together and achieved harmony, and trees, grasses, birds, and beasts appeared. Mago continued to develop the Earth into a beautiful home for life through the energy of Yullyeo. She entrusted the four pairs of humans with one task each to perform on the Earth. The Yellows supervised earth; the Whites, air; the Blacks, fire; and the Blues, water. Over the course of several generations, the population of Mago Castle grew to 12,000.

All of those at Mago Castle lived in harmony as they drank the earth milk. Their character was harmonious, warm, pure, and clear. They listened to the music of Heaven, could go wherever they wanted, and could even move without showing themselves.

When they finished their work and the world was bathed in golden light, they would talk with each other even in silence. Moving beyond the limitations of their finite physical bodies, they all enjoyed long life because they were one with heaven and earth. Until just before the Fall . . .

As the number of people grew, however, there was not enough earth milk to go around, and they had to wait their turn to drink it. There were those who felt hungry. One day, one of them ate a grape and experienced a great change. Using the five flavors of the grape as a metaphor, the *Budoji* expresses it as the "Fall of the Five Flavors": bitter, sour, sweet, salty, and pungent.

As others started to eat grapes, they lost their sense of absolute unity. They came to think of themselves as different from each other and their eyes opened to the great multitude of things in the world. The people of Mago Castle started to discriminate between right and wrong, clean and unclean, and correct and incorrect.

They started to separate in their minds the concepts of body, mind, and soul, which before had been connected. They lost their ability to commune directly with Yullyeo as well as their sense of unity with other beings. Fighting and conflict developed, and the order and harmony of Mago Castle were shattered.

The leaders of the Yellow, White, Black, and Blue tribes, taking collective responsibility for what had happened, decided to take their descendants and leave Mago Castle. They were worried that Mago Castle itself would be destroyed if they remained. Leaving the castle, each group went its own way—east, west, north, and south. Before departing, though, they resolved as a group to recover their lost divinity and return to Mago Castle one day. This is the "Vow of Restoration."

To return to Mago Castle, they engaged in a practice for recovering their divinity by training their ki energy, which is the source of all things visible and invisible. That practice has come down to us as the traditional Korean system of mind-body training called "Sundo," which I have modernized as Dahn Yoga and Brain Education.

My understanding is that Mago Castle is not a physical place but a symbol of the state of human consciousness and energy that is completely one with divinity. In that sense, Mago Castle is inside us.

In this tale of Mago Castle, I found the part about the "Vow of Restoration" deeply moving, for it shows us what human beings—deep down inside—really want to become and where they want to return. Humans are fundamentally spiritual beings. That is why they ceaselessly thirst for divinity and seek to become one with it.

Though we may have plenty to eat, a cool car, an amazing house, and people we love, still we search for this divinity. We have a desire for something that lasts even longer than our finite, personal lives; a thirst to know some world greater than what we see, hear, and feel; and a desire to satisfy the thirst of our souls, which is unquenchable no matter how many things we possess.

Another thing I want to share with the readers of this book, along with the tale of Mago, involves the ChunBuKyung. The ChunBuKyung is an ancient scripture of Korea that is

reportedly about 10,000 years old. Contained in its short text of no more than eighty-one characters are the principles of the creation, evolution, and completion of the cosmos.

I first came across the ChunBuKyung about thirty years ago, after I attained enlightenment on Moak Mountain. Even now, I remember vividly the shock and deep emotion I felt at the time, for within those eighty-one characters was fully expressed the true nature of life that I had seen through my enlightenment.

The most common among the eighty-one characters of the ChunBuKyung is the figure that means "One," and it contains the very heart of the ChunBuKyung. In the ChunBuKyung, this "One" is eternal life, existing without beginning and without end; it refers to the source of being from which all things emerge and to which all things return.

Those who have realized the meaning of this "One" come to know that their own lives, as well as the lives of others, are rooted in the One, the Source of all existence. When we awaken to the meaning of this One, we can see that our separate, individual selves are an illusion and that all organisms and, moreover, everything in existence can be viewed as flowers blooming on the one tree called "life."

We gain the ability to see a world in which, despite differneces, all are one and the Source of all is one.

In the ChunBuKyung, we find the verse, "The Original Mind is bright like the sun, and so searches for brightness itself." This means that all human beings have a bright divine nature and long to become one with that nature; we can understand it in the same context as the Vow of Restoration in the tale of Mago Castle.

We all have a divine nature and we have a thirst to become one with that divinity. That divinity lets us find meaning in life even at the pinnacle of happiness, lets us weep for the pain and sorrow of others, and lets us dream of a more beautiful world.

19 THE STORY OF LIFEPARTICLES AND THE MINDSCREEN

AFTER I CAME TO know that my essence is Chunjikiun (cosmic energy) and Chunjimaum (cosmic mind) on Moak Mountain in Korea thirty years ago, even now the question of how to communicate this enlightenment to many people still remains. The reason is because I believe that a realization like this can simultaneously enable people to solve their personal problems as well as participate in the great cause of actualizing Earth peace.

In order to find ways to popularize that enlightenment, I've conducted research constantly for the past thirty years while developing and sharing various meditation and training methods. Among these modalities, Brain Education, Dahn Yoga, and Brain Wave Vibration are the most widely known. What I've been focusing on recently, though, and wish to share with readers through this book, are LifeParticles and the MindScreen.

LifeParticles and the MindScreen are different names for Chunjikiun and Chunjimaum. Even though I'd used these two concepts for so long, the reason I had to develop new ones is because human consciousness is changing rapidly and becoming integrated through the influence of information communication methods that are evolving at incredible speeds.

I believe that humanity has now reached the Shinmyung Era. "Shinmyung" is a Korean word referring to brightened awareness and awakened consciousness. Thus, the Shinmyung Era is the phase in the development of human society when we enter into our greatest collective spiritual maturity. Humanity has begun to realize that a high quality of life must include self-realization beyond material values. Many people are now focusing on harmonious coexistence among human cultures. Both personally and collectively, people are making an effort to integrate seemingly conflicting elements such as matter and spirit, yin and yang, human and nature, and God and human.

It feels as if we're watching from the sidelines without being able to do anything. The earth is up to its neck in this crisis of civilization. The clock of civilization is moving much faster than all of us expected, and the Earth's environment is losing its balance at a shocking rate.

The only way we can make the global changes that we want is for each and every one of us to realize his or her responsibility for the earth and humanity and to take action.

I believe that anyone who has a spiritual sense has the ability to understand the main point of LifeParticles and the MindScreen, whether or not they have practiced meditation; utilizing this can demonstrate incredible creative power that will result in a collective change in consciousness.

LifeParticles and the MindScreen are concepts that I created through the power of imagination. The spiritual sensitivity of humans in the digital era will naturally give rise to the Shinmyung Era only if we make good choices about how we use our brains. I created these training tools to assist in this evolution because I have a deep sense of urgency about human consciousness, which I believe must awaken quickly on a large scale. The time is now or never.

I think of LifeParticles as the most elemental particles that comprise the universe, the smallest particles that transmit information and life. Because this is a concept that came out of the insight I gained through meditation, there is no way to prove it scientifically; but I hope and I also believe that science will someday come to the same discovery.

LifeParticles, which vibrate at infinitely varied frequencies, gather and disperse in countless ways to create innumerable life phenomena. They not only fill the entire universe from the visible physical world to the invisible spiritual world, but also go beyond the limitations of time and space. In effect, they can move freely to any time or place. From a visual perspective, LifeParticles are expressed as grains of brightly shining light or as a light powder. The experience of the Crystal Palace at Bell Rock that I described earlier in this book was the experience of how my body disintegrated into LifeParticles and became one with the infinite energy of the universe.

The MindScreen is a spatial representation of an awakened consciousness. The MindScreen is not a flat surface on which images are projected. It has dimension, like a hologram, and at the same time is the infinite internal space where all mental activity takes place. The MindScreen is basically what you focus your awareness on as reflected by an image in your brain. It is a space of infinite creation and potential that is unrestricted by time and space. It can become infinitely big; inside of it, we can move freely between the past, present, and future. The MindScreen is the space where LifeParticles are active, the passage through which they travel, and at the same time, the governing body that transports the LifeParticles.

What is important to recognize is that, in the end, the MindScreen is also a function of our brain. I've had a deep interest in the brain for a long time, and I have conducted much research on how the creative ability possessed by the brain could be utilized to the utmost.

When it comes to the brain, many people feel that it's unfamiliar and think of it as the exclusive property of doctors or scientists. We think, speak, and move through our brain. With our brain, we love, dream dreams, make plans for the future, and ask ourselves, "Who am I?" Our brain is the place where dreams and reality, the divine and the human, and matter and spirit come together.

That's why I feel that anyone who wants to live a more creative and worthwhile life has to know about their brain and the principles and methods of utilizing it. I believe the human brain has an innate yearning to experience becoming one with divinity. For this reason, I took Korean Sundo philosophy and mind-body training methods and grafted them to Western neuroscience in order to create Brain Education.

One of the ancient sacred texts of Korean Sundo, the SamIlShinGo, contains this phrase: "Look for God inside your True Self. God has already descended into and resides in your brain." This amazing message has been passed down for more than 10,000 years. In the Sundo tradition, it has been reconfirmed through many spiritual teachers who pursued human completion through independent study. I believe this message is the hope of humanity. The goal of all of the training methods I have developed and shared until now, regardless of differences in external techniques, is for all people to ultimately realize and recover the divinity in their own brain.

The MindScreen is the most highly developed function of our brain. The vast majority of people are unable to utilize their brain's ability beyond their knowledge or experience. However, our brain is able to do what we request, even if it's something we've never done before or even something we don't know. Our brain has great creative power that looks for a path if it doesn't see one—and makes one if it can't find one. Through our MindScreen, we can go beyond the limitations of knowledge and experience not only to draw out the great potential our brain has, but also use it.

While looking for ways to help more people fully understand and utilize LifeParticles and the MindScreen, I realized I could express the two concepts as images. I felt that images could convey my intended meaning more easily and quickly than spoken words or written text.

I asked an artist to paint the image of LifeParticles according to my description of the image I had seen in a state of deep meditation. The brilliant red light shown radiating powerfully from the center is the LifeParticle Sun. This Sun emanates a steady stream of LifeParticles that revives and heals all creation. The Sun in the painting represents the purest, clearest energy, which is the source of love and creative power. Even a novice practitioner of meditation can resonate with the highest level of energy waves in the universe by bringing to mind the image of the LifeParticle Sun.

The MindScreen image is a representation of an experience I had while meditating on the top of Bell Rock. In my mind's eye, I traveled down into the beautiful Crystal Palace located below the red rock formation. At that time, I could sense a powerful stream of energy penetrating my entire body. Although my body was sitting at the top of Bell Rock, I entered into a state of consciousness through which I was able to see and feel my body, Bell Rock, and the entire universe all at the same time. In other words, my third eye, located between the eyebrows, was widely open throughout the experience. The MindScreen image offers visual inspiration to help anyone open their third eye as I did in that meditation.

It is important to realize that you are fundamentally made up of LifeParticles, as is everyone else. Please realize that you, like everyone you meet, possess a MindScreen. Making use of this powerful asset will help you cultivate a healthier, happier, and more peaceful life, and it will help you do the same for others. This book's appendix contains a meditation method that will help you make the most of your MindScreen and LifeParticles.

20 DISCOVER THE GREATNESS WITHIN

Have you ever thought of yourself as a great being? Have you ever been deeply moved by a thought that came from inside?

One day, I heard a voice inside me that was sincerely concerned for the future of the earth and humanity. That voice asked, *Would a world where all life forms on this earth live together in peace and harmony be impossible?* That voice answered, *If all people really wanted that and chose that kind of world, why wouldn't it come true?*

That voice moved me deeply and made me go to great pains to figure out what I could do for this earth and for humanity. I was beautifully moved when I did that. That feeling was very deep and true and it led me to choose a completely different course for my life than I had up until

that point. That one thought and choice changed me and changed my life.

When I heard the voice say I had a mission to awaken the consciousness of many people, I was well aware, in light of that great mission, of my many shortcomings. However, I did not deny that voice. Nor did I shrink back because of my shortcomings. I believed that if this path were truly the way of heaven, then it would open to me on its own. That was the truth.

Certainly, there were other voices that tried to shake my resolve. They echoed inside of me as well as echoing on the outside. However, human beings are capable of distinguishing between their true voice and their false voices. Everyone has this ability. It's just that not all people choose to listen to and act upon their true voice. I tried hard to follow my true voice, even in instances where it seemed unrealistic.

What inner voice are you listening to now? It just might be that you're hearing a mission from that voice that feels too big for you if compared to your own measurement of yourself. *Watch out.* Along with that voice, you will hear many voices that will try to make you into a very small being. There may even be a cynical voice that's saying, "Be realistic," and pretending to be you. *Don't waver.*

Even if certain suffering is in the future, you have to take the path that your real True Self wants. Until you take that path, your soul will feel its thirst forever.

I think every person hears that kind of inner voice at least several times in their life. And I also believe that, rather than pursuing only their own personal profit, all people have an inherent desire to be of service to their family and neighbors and, beyond that, to their entire community and to humanity. I call that the "greatness within." From that greatness, the beautiful and holy intention to benefit all life springs forth.

At the moment you heard your inner voice, what did you do? At the moment you became aware of your greatness within, what did you do? Did you acknowledge and accept it? Or did you turn away from it?

Each of us is a great life and a great soul. When the one holy thought to do something widely beneficial to the world comes out, we need to have the eyes to perceive it, the courage to accept and choose it, and the will to put it into action. In the process of cherishing that one thought and pouring all our devotion into it, we can create true change in the lives of ourselves and humanity.

Human beings appear briefly in time and space and then disappear. Everyone dies in the end. From the perspective of the universe, one human living and dying and one fly living and dying are incidents of more or less the same gravity. The universe will not be sadder for you because you died instead of a fly.

Does that mean that human life is futile? No, that's not true. On a certain day, we receive this life as a gift. As we receive that gift, we also receive with it the gift of infinite freedom of choice to make it completely our own. We can live as we choose, and we can even determine the meaning of that life for ourselves.

Life is not meaningless. However, if you don't listen to the voice of your True Self and discover a dream into which you can pour all your passion, all you can do is keep living with a feeling of futility in the midst of a mindlessly hectic lifestyle. You've probably asked yourself this question at the end of the day: Did I live well today? At that time, with what standard did you answer? If you don't have a dream, if you don't have a value that lends meaning to your life, then you will not be able to answer this question even when you have completed your life and gone to your eternal resting place. *Did I live my life well?*

Dreams are reality that has not yet become true. However, in the hearts of some people, they have already come true. People whose dreams are already achieved in their heart and can see that as they boldly throw themselves into it—these are people with true courage. Life isn't about sticking to predetermined conventions. It's not like life exists somewhere in the form of a manufactured good and you're supposed to discover it. Life is about following the voice of your True Self and "inventing" it as something all your own.

Do you have a dream? If you do, what is it? Is your dream similar to mine? I hope that even more people dream the same dream as me, because my dream is so big I couldn't handle it by myself.

If you are someone who has the same dream as me, this is what I want to say to you. Right now, you are planting a single tree. Right now, you are sowing a single seed. And you are beginning to knit something with one strand of yarn. The first step or two are nothing, but imagine that you continue that work for ten years. One tree becomes a forest, one seed becomes a field, and that single thread becomes a beautiful cloth. Believe in the life inside you, believe in the great and holy mind within you, and push forward with the dream you have chosen until you make it.

I wrote this book according to the message and inspiration that arose from within. If my stories provide you with any inspiration, then believe in that and trust it. And live according to how that inspiration and feeling move you. Express it and communicate it to other people. Let the greatness inside of all people awaken together and respond in kind.

When everyone resonates with the holiness and greatness within, we can overcome personal limitations and create mature change for the future of the earth. I do not mean just one or two great individuals, but the birth of a great humanity—this is the only hope of the earth.

Until now, humanity has pursued material success as a primary value. I believe that humanity must now pursue completion of the soul as a central value. The definition of success is relative and requires arbitrary judgments that compare one person to another; completion, however, is absolute, and based on a standard derived from your own native conscience. Success, as society usually defines it, is achieved by acquiring wealth and fame, but completion is achieved by knowing the purpose of your life and living a life that's loyal to that calling. Success is a dog-eat-dog race, but completion is an event where each person prepares their own victory trophy. While success in human society requires competition with other people, spiritual completion is instead about helping others. Completion requires continuous self-reflection and self-motivation for personal improvement.

In Sedona, where it's springtime now, wildflowers are blooming here and there. Some are large and some are small; some wither quickly while others last longer. There are the charming little yellow Mexican Poppies, the magnificent white Evening Primroses, and the fiery red Indian Paintbrushes. Their shapes and colors are all unique.

Looking at the wildflowers, we don't assume that the large flowers are necessarily more beautiful than the smaller ones. Nor do we think that the flowers that stay in bloom longer are somehow more excellent than the ones that fade more quickly. Large flowers are simply large, and small flowers are simply small. There is no reason to say that a flower that blooms longer is better than one that withers earlier. These things are just a matter of diversity, not an indication of superiority.

Each individual wildflower blossom that colors Sedona's springtime is beautiful. More importantly, they all contribute to something that equals more than the sum of their parts. In Sedona there are large flowers, small flowers, flowers in full bloom, and flowers that have not yet bloomed. Some flowers are already wilted while others dance proudly in the breeze. Sedona's red earth embraces the roots of the wildflowers and cradles an assortment of variously shaped rocks. The bright azure sky acts as a backdrop for the flowers, the juniper trees, and the red rocks. All these things work together in perfect harmony to create the stunning beauty that Sedona offers.

We are individual flowers blooming on a single tree called Life. Because each flower makes the effort to complete its own unique color, shape, and fragrance, the whole tree of Life can emanate greater vital power in all its fullness. Though we are all one, we each have our unique individuality, but we also share the same origin. No one is dropped into the universe all alone; there is no separation between personal completion and collective completion. People who realize this choose a life devoted to collective harmony and not just to their own happiness.

Because everyone has a natural yearning for completion, we are able to change and recreate ourselves endlessly. I believe that we all have an internal guidance system that gives us constant motivation to move toward completion. Because we have a sense of completion within us, and because we have the will and desire to reach that state of completion, human beings have the potential for greatness and can become greater at any time.

21 The Sedona Spirit

Around mid-April of this year, I climbed to the top of Bell Rock for the first time in a very long time. Although when I first settled in Sedona I would go sometimes twice a day, in recent years I haven't had many opportunities to climb Bell Rock. The warm afternoon sunlight shining down welcomed me as it always has. When I was almost at the top, I noticed the blue sky without a spot of cloud between the red rocks that stood tall. My heart leapt as though it were the first time I'd ever seen that.

As the sun started to set, it stained Courthouse Butte next to Bell Rock with gold. The branches of the pine trees swayed gently in the evening wind. That day, I meditated for a long time at the top of Bell Rock and thought of the millions of tourists that come to Sedona.

I suddenly thought of how the people who come to Sedona are like salmon returning to the river where they were born during the spawning season. Salmon are born in a river and go to the ocean. Salmon that have lived in the ocean for three or four years return to their home river where they were born when it's time for them to lay their eggs. There are times when the journey is so difficult that their whole body becomes beaten to a pulp as they give their all to swim upriver. Salmon that have gone in search of the source of life like that, and returned to their home river, lay their eggs and then either go back to the ocean or die there.

There are a lot of people who come to Sedona from neighboring cities like Phoenix, Tucson, or Los Angeles, but far more people come from all over North America or from as far away as Asia or Europe. What calls those people to Sedona?

There are probably a vast variety of superficial reasons as to why each person comes; but I think there also exists a certain yearning that makes them head toward Sedona, like salmon returning to the river where they were born. People who come to Sedona aren't coming simply to look at the beautiful views. They want to experience something new, such as adventure or inspiration. I believe the yearning that seeks to bring something new to a life that's lost its luster is an inherently spiritual thing.

That day, after I came down from Bell Rock, I named what people coming to Sedona are looking for—the "Sedona spirit." And then, when I thought about it, I saw that the certain power that drew me to Sedona fifteen years ago, the essence of all the things that I experienced in Sedona, was also the "Sedona spirit."

If you are living in Sedona or if you have ever visited, what would you pick out as the essence of the Sedona spirit? I would pick out three things. I want to tell the visitors of Sedona to feel the following three things and, through whatever it may take, make them their own.

More than anything else, the Sedona spirit is the spirit of creation. The primordial beauty of nature in Sedona and its sky and red rocks that, depending on the light of the desert sun, change with such diversity, awakens a great creativity within us. No matter what difficult situations we may find ourselves in, we are able to change them and create them anew according to our choice. We can choose hope, no matter what the situation. With amazing creativity, we can design our lives and become the drivers of our destiny.

The Sedona spirit is the spirit of interacting with the earth. The sky that opens so wide and deep above the red rocks, the juniper trees and cacti that emanate vital power, the golden full moon that cuts through the desert night . . . all these environments help us to feel the earth as a life form and allow energetic and spiritual interactions with the earth. The experience of interacting with the earth connects us with a greater and more permanent power beyond the limited and finite self to bring us spiritual fulfillment and a sense of unity. It leads us naturally as members of the planet Earth to earth-centered living in which we coexist with all life.

I would like to call the characteristics of a new lifestyle that pursues the Sedona spirit "Awakened Living." The essence of Awakened Living is that it doesn't separate the spiritual from daily life. The age in which we look for spirituality deep in a mountain or in mystical doctrines is over. In the here and now, where our work, people, and passion are tied closely together—I believe that is the true spiritual lifestyle.

For Awakened Living, you need wisdom that doesn't necessarily coincide with a religion or value system that systematizes spirituality. The most important questions in life are not answered by experts or by systems. They can help us on our journey to ask those questions but finding the answers is always our own to do. We are the one and only experts, writers, and authorities of our own lives.

Over the past thirty years, I've studied, developed, and taught innumerable self-help methods and meditation techniques. Lately, however, I've been saying, "Don't just do training." Instead, I say, "Practice living or live practice." Setting aside thirty minutes to one hour a day in order to meditate is valuable. But it's important to let the power of your meditation last throughout your day.

Meditation isn't only for quieting and relaxing the mind or for comforting a body tired from a day's work. Meditation is about living your life in the here and now. One of the most important goals of meditation is to create the kind of life you want. It can be as simple as going through your day with a focused purpose, or periodically stopping to take a few deep breaths. By helping you to have clearer intentions and make better choices in every moment, all forms of meditation allow you to realize you are the author of each moment and can manifest your own greatness anywhere and anytime.

If you have come to Sedona, don't forget to take these three elements of the Sedona spirit into your life. In the phrase "Sedona spirit," Sedona doesn't just mean a land of red rocks located in northern Arizona. Sedona is a space of infinite creation in your heart, your greatest dream, and the most sacred moments of your life. And it is the power of your choice to choose hope even in the most difficult moments.

Epilogue

MY EYES OPEN BY themselves early every morning around three or four o'clock. The first thing I do when I get up in the morning is to sit quietly, steady my breath, and open my MindScreen. Through the MindScreen, I listen to the voice of my inner self and interact with the heart of the earth.

If I follow my breath and ride the rhythm of life and go deep into my inner self, the boundaries that separate my body and my surroundings disappear and I encounter infinite empty space filled with LifeParticles, the grains of brightly shining light. At that moment, I can feel infinite love and responsibility toward all creation flowing out from a sense of complete oneness.

I express my gratitude for having been granted another day, and I meditate and pray about how I will use this life allotted to me and for what. I pray for the people that I love and am concerned for, my dream and vision, and for all life.

I offer my reverence to the divine quality of the universe that permits us to feel love, joy, and infinite creativity.

Whenever I bring Sedona to mind, there is a dream that always spreads before me. It's an image of all the people who come to Sedona interacting with the heart of the earth and becoming aware of the great spirit and strength within themselves. I also see these people each returning to their lives, actualizing that realization and sharing it together as they cultivate themselves and their communities more beautifully. I draw on my MindScreen the image of the inspiration and message that Sedona gave to me, and let it spread to the whole world, just as the invisible vortex energy of Sedona spreads out to the whole earth.

No matter from where in the world I'm returning, in Sedona I always feel a sense of safety and peace, as if I've returned to the home of my soul and the arms of Mother Earth and the red land that always welcomes me with open arms. I have not yet been able to fully repay the debt I owe to Sedona, which has given to me so generously. I believe that the only way to repay that debt is for me to deliver the message I received from Sedona and the heart of the earth with more and more people until the final moment of my life.

Finally, I would like to share with you a poem that I wrote as I thought about the message.

Sedona Message

Whatever the path that brought you here
There is a reason why you came,
Though you may not realize it now.
Therefore, please open your ears.
Listen to the message that Sedona has for you.
The old juniper standing tall in the golden sunset
    just might tell you the reason.

Whatever fork in the road of life you stand at now
There is a question in your heart,
Though you may not realize it now.
Therefore, please open your ears.
Listen to the message that Sedona has for you.
The red rock that resembles the face of a Native
    American just might help you remember that
    question.

Whatever the question growing in your heart
You can find the answer to that question within
    yourself,
Though you may not realize it now.
So, please open your ears.
Listen to the message that Sedona has for you.
The rushing water of Oak Creek, shimmering
    under a full moon, just might give you the
    answer.

When the long howl of a coyote weaves its way
   through a night sky brimming with stars
When the afternoon monsoon shakes Thunder
   Mountain with thunder and lightning
There is a message from Sedona that calls to you
   with a roar far greater.

There is a world all living creatures have dreamed
   of together ever since the Earth came to be.
There is a world dreamed of by Mago, Mother
   Earth, and human beings, the heavens and
   the Earth, the mountains and the sea.
The old juniper tree, the red rocks, and the
   rushing water of Oak Creek share a dream.
Oh, friend who has come to Sedona, take this
   dream with you.

This dream is the reason why you have come to
   this place, and it just might be your question
   and your answer.
This dream just might awaken the greatest things
   within you.
A new Heaven, a new Earth, a new people, and a
   new life path,
A world of peace in which all life is harmonious
   in a sacred Heaven and an abundant Earth.
Though you may not realize it now, you are a
   being that has come to the Earth to turn this
   dream into a reality.

APPENDIX I

SEDONA VORTEX
MEDITATION GUIDE

APPENDIX II

LifeParticles and the
MindScreen Meditation

SEDONA VORTEX
MEDITATION GUIDE

IN THIS SECTION, I will introduce some simple meditation exercises you can practice at the major vortexes of
Sedona. You may do them either alone or with the help
of an experienced guide. Feel free to practice these exercises in locations other than the particular one mentioned.
For example, you may practice the Bell Rock Meditation
at Airport Mesa, Boynton Canyon, or any of the other
vortexes. They can also be used effectively in places other
than Sedona. When your senses are fully awakened and
you are aware of your inner self, you will be able to sense
what you need at a certain location. You will intuitively
know which meditation suits a given situation at a given
time.

PREPARATION EXERCISE
FEELING KI ENERGY

Feeling ki (energy) is the most basic step in Sedona Vortex Meditations. If you haven't yet experienced energy, I recommend that you first try feeling it through this exercise. As you develop your ability to sense energy with your body, it will become easier for you to connect with the energy of Sedona's vortexes.

Humans consist of a visible physical body and an invisible consciousness. Energy is the medium that constantly exchanges information between the physical body and the world of consciousness. Energy is what connects the body and the mind. As your experience deepens, you will come to realize that the body and consciousness are also ultimately made of energy.

Sit comfortably with your eyes closed and your back straight. Rub your hands together or shake them out for about thirty seconds to awaken their senses.

Place your hands on your knees with your palms facing upward. Breathe steadily and comfortably. Keeping your palms facing upward, raise your hands very slowly, about five inches above your knees, and then lower them back down about three inches. Repeat the motion of raising and lowering your hands several times. Focus your awareness on your palms. Imagine energy continuously coming into your palms from the air. You'll get a heavy feeling in your hands. That is the feeling of energy.

Now slowly bring your hands in front of your chest with your palms facing each other. Leave about two inches of space in between your palms and focus your awareness on your hands. Very slowly, move your hands apart from each other and focus on the sensation in the palms. When you have moved them a few inches farther apart, slowly begin to bring them back to the original position again. As you continue to move your hands closer and farther apart, feel the energy field that exists between them. Focus on the presence between the palms, imagining that your hands are linked together with energy.

Now imagine there is an energy ball in between your hands. Imagine that you are grasping the ball of energy and rotate the ball by turning your hands in opposite directions to each other. Expand the ball by drawing your hands slowly outward, and then bring your hands closer together again, making the ball of energy smaller and more concentrated. Continue to concentrate on the energy sensation between your hands as you grow and shrink the ball between your hands.

Now lower your hands slowly to your knees and then breathe in and out.

What sensations did you feel in your hands? There are a variety of sensations you may have experienced, including your palms growing warmer, a tingling sensation of electricity in your fingers, or a feeling of magnetism, as if each palm were a magnet. They might feel like they have equivalent polarity, pushing each other apart, or they might feel like they have opposite polarity, pulling each other together. When feeling energy between your hands, it is important to remember to focus your awareness on your hands. Even if you go through the physical motions, you will not be able to fully feel energy if your mind is wandering.

Feeling energy indicates that your awareness is in your body, your thoughts have quieted, and your brainwaves are steady. When you have reached a state of relaxed concentration, your body will become relaxed but your consciousness will remain alert. In this state, your body responds optimally to the vortexes and allows your body and mind to undergo more diverse, profound energy transformation.

When your ability to sense energy deepens, this exercise eventually progresses into a beautiful energy dance in which your hands and body slowly move and naturally follow the flow of energy. When your energy in your body becomes more powerful, your movements develop further to acquire martial arts elements, like those of kigong or tai chi.

It is best to awaken the senses in your body and mind through energy sensitization like that presented here before you engage in the Sedona Vortex training and meditation.

BELL ROCK
FEELING A VORTEX

This meditation is meant to open your blocked energy points and meridians by connecting the swirling vortex energy to your body. It can be done sitting or standing; beginners may find the standing posture more convenient.

Stand with your legs about shoulder width apart and release all tension from your body. With your eyes closed, scan each part of your body with your imagination: the crown of your head . . . face . . . neck . . . shoulders . . . chest . . . solar plexus . . . lower abdomen . . . hip joints . . . thighs . . . knees . . . ankles . . . and the bottom of the feet. With a relaxed body and mind, keep focusing your awareness on your body.

Now bring your awareness to the bottom of your feet. Imagine strong vortex energy rising up under your feet from the red rock of Bell Rock and swirling up in a spiral shape in and around your body.

The energy rises up past your feet, past your knees, hip joints, and lower back. Surrender your body to the spiraling movement. Your knees rotate in a circular motion. Your shoulders and arms make circles, too. Quiet your thinking mind and surrender your body to the energy, letting your body move as it desires.

All of your joints draw circles and rotate—your ankles, knees, hip joints, lower back, shoulders, elbows, wrists, and neck. With every movement of your joints, imagine the

powerful healing energy of the vortex coming into your joints while the negative, stagnant energy leaves your body. If you have pain or discomfort in any part of your body, focus more on those areas. When you become connected with the vortex's powerful healing energy, your body's natural healing power will become activated and your muscles and bones can realign.

When you want to get rid of the thoughts and emotions that taunt you, keep moving your body and breathe out deeply while saying "hoo." The negative energy will leave with your exhalation.

When you reach the point where you feel your body has become free and comfortable, slowly stop your movement. You may feel as if your feet are stuck to the rock. The healing energy of the red earth travels through your feet, up your spine, and straight up through the crown of your head. Imagine bright, sacred energy from the sky coming down through the crown of your head, down your spine, through your feet, and into the ground. Energy from heaven comes down through the crown of your head, and energy from the earth rises from under your feet. Picture a solid column of energy at the center of your body connecting heaven and earth.

CATHEDRAL ROCK
PURIFYING EMOTIONS

First, find an adequate spot to engage in meditation. Try to find a quiet location on the rock next to the creek where you can hear the sound of the water. Before you start the meditation, do some stretches or release tension from your body by standing with knees slightly bent and bouncing up and down gently until your whole body relaxes.

Sit on the rock in a half-lotus position, close your eyes, and make your back straight. Place your hands on your knees with your palms facing up. Relax your body and mind and steady your breath. Slowly lift your hands about five inches above your knees. Imagine a soft energy from the atmosphere coming down into your palms. This soft and gentle energy comes down into your head, shoulders, chest, and palms, and purifies your emotions.

Focus your awareness on your chest. You may feel a particular emotion or recall a certain memory from the past. Loneliness, sorrow, anxiety, longing, anger . . . whatever emotion it is, do not hold on to it. Rather, just let yourself feel it. You may remember a past memory related to this emotion. You may now intentionally bring up any memories or emotions that you wish to release and bid farewell.

Now, let's clear these emotions and memories that have been burdening you. Bring your attention to the sound of the trickling water. Rather than listening with your ears, imagine you are listening with your whole body. Now imagine the clear water trickling into the crown of your head and flowing down into your heart. Imagine it cleanly washing away the memories you want to let go along with the emotions that have caused you to suffer. Slowly move your head and torso from side to side, moving like a reed swaying in the wind, and keep washing away the energy of your outdated emotions with the sound of the water.

Now slowly submerge both hands in the water. Imagine that the emotions in your heart are passing through your arms and out through the tips of your fingers. Send the emotions that have made you suffer down the river. As the heavy emotions and memories leave, feel the emotions of forgiveness, gratitude, and love filling your heart.

After that, sit comfortably, straighten your lower back, and accumulate energy in your lower abdomen. Breathe comfortably while focusing on the feeling of energy accumulating in your lower abdomen. Keep breathing slowly, deeply, and softly.

AIRPORT MESA
STARLIGHT MEDITATION

Airport Mesa is a great place to do sunrise or sunset meditation. When meditating at sunset, I recommend the Chakra Light Meditation on page 200 to awaken your chakras through the golden light of the setting sun. In the following meditation, I will introduce Starlight Meditation, which is best to do at night in the summer.

On a clear night, when you can see the sky filled with stars, choose a spot with even ground somewhere on Airport Mesa and lie down comfortably. Use a towel or yoga mat if desired. Then lift your gaze toward the sky.

When was the last time you looked face to face at the sky? The stars sparkle like jewels scattered upon black velvet, and it seems as though they might come showering down at any moment. When you lie under the night sky in Sedona, time will feel grander than it usually feels and it will seem as though the sky is far greater and more expansive than before. You may be overcome with the vibrant feeling of existing as a single life form in this great, vast universe.

Now slowly lift your hands and reach as if you were trying to touch the sky. Imagine that the stars crumble into gold dust and come into your fingers and hands. It feels as if your hands are hanging in thin air. Feel the energy of the starlight come into your hands, and then to your arms, shoulders, and chest. Keep feeling the energy of the starlight coming into your body and let your body ride the energy, moving your hands slowly as if you were dancing with the stars. The energy of the starlight fills your entire body.

Choose one bright star that resonates most in your heart. Now slowly overlap your hands over your lower abdomen. Close your eyes and imagine that star slowly falling toward you. The starlight goes through your forehead and into your head.

That starlight comes into your head and awakens your divinity. It will feel as if your head is filled completely with bright light. Now ask the star, "Who am I?" What does the star tell you? Tell the star what is in your heart and listen carefully to what the star says to you. The infinite life energy of the universe is coming down to your body. Breathe comfortably and deeply as you receive this life energy that is so abundant throughout the universe. Feel the life energy in your body growing more and more.

OAK CREEK CANYON
WATER SOUND SELF-HEALING

Sit comfortably in a quiet location where you can hear the sound of the creek. Close your eyes, straighten your back, and breathe steadily. Open the senses of your body and focus on the sounds you hear. You can hear the sound of the creek. Focus on this sound with a relaxed mind and you will hear the sound of the water flow more clearly—as if it were closer than it is.

Imagine that the water flows through your whole body from the top of your head to your toes. You may feel the water run through your body freely with no obstruction; or you may feel that the water does not flow as easily in certain parts where there may be energy blockages—perhaps in your head, shoulders, chest, or solar plexus. These areas are in need of better energy circulation, so give them more focused attention during the meditation.

Bring your awareness to the crown of your head. Clear water from the creek is continuing to pour onto the crown of your head and is flowing into your head. Bring your awareness to your brain. The negative thoughts and energy in your brain are being washed away with the clear water. Now, the clear water washes down your face, neck, and straight through your chest. It continues to flow through your forehead . . . eyes . . . nose . . . mouth . . . chin . . . neck . . . and chest.

Focus on your chest, visualizing all of your heavy emotional energy being washed away with the water.

Now bring your awareness to your torso and inner organs. In the East, our organs and emotions are believed to have an intimate connection to each other. Allow the sound vibrations of the water to seep through your organs and wash away the energies of stagnant emotions: heart . . . lungs . . . stomach . . . liver . . . kidneys . . . large intestines . . . small intestines . . . stay with each organ for about one minute as you imagine the sound of the fresh water cleanly purifying that organ. Now, the water flows down your lower back and waist, past your hips, and down your legs. From the crown of your head, down to the tips of your toes, inside and outside your body, all of the negative energy is being cleanly washed away.

PRAYER

The simple yet holy atmosphere of the Chapel of the Holy Cross moves many to pray. Light a candle inside the chapel and offer the sincerest prayer in your heart. No matter where you choose to pray, the following will help you in your prayer.

Presence: Allow your body and mind to completely be present in the moment. Do not let the past or future or thoughts of things you should have done before or should do later tag along.

Peace: Offer your prayer with a peaceful heart. The purpose of your prayer should be peaceful, of course. However, even more important is that your mind remains peaceful at the moment when you offer your prayer. There are times when people pray from a place of greed, fear, jealousy, and hatred. When such emotions arise, pray that peace will return to your heart.

Alignment: Seek spiritual, energetic, and physical alignment. On the spiritual level, observe whether your prayer is coming from a heart of peace and love. To align yourself energetically, breathe deeply and comfortably while feeling the energy in your whole body as you offer your prayer. Align yourself physically by straightening your back and maintaining a proper sacred posture.

Sincerity: The more real your prayer feels to you, the deeper your prayer will be. What will you feel once your prayer is realized? Experience that very feeling in that particular moment, as if it has already come true.

Constancy: As you pray, voices of doubt or fear may disturb your mind's composure. Denying, arguing with, or ignoring these voices is not helpful. Instead, accept them as they are, feel them, and breathe out while saying, "I return you to the origin of life." If needed, you can repeat this several times. As the negative voices die down, you will feel your mind recover its composure.

Gratitude: We pray because we wish to fulfill a dream or wish. These dreams fill our lives with passion and creativity. When you pray, offer your gratitude for having the opportunity to do so. Allow this gratitude to completely fill your heart.

SCHNEBLY HILL
CHAKRA LIGHT MEDITATION

Schnebly Hill is a great place to practice Chakra Light Meditation. When you sit on the hill called Merry-Go-Round, you can see formations fittingly nicknamed "Cow Pies" in the distance and tall red rocks surrounding you on either side and behind you. As you sit in the midst of all this, you feel as though you are meeting "one on one" with the sun as you bathe in its penetrating light.

Light Meditation is a powerful exercise that can awaken the body's chakras. Breathing is the most important aspect of Chakra Light Meditation. Through your breath, you can bring life energy into your body to activate every chakra.

The best times to practice Light Meditation are during sunrise or sunset. The sunlight at these times of the day will activate the pituitary and pineal glands in your brain, and boost your spiritual energy to its fullest.

We will start with Chakra Color Meditation, which uses the natural colors of Sedona.

First take a moment to loosen up your body and then sit down in a half-lotus position. Straighten your back, and with your palms facing upward, place them on your knees. With your eyes closed, release tension from your shoulders and chest, and calm your breathing as you relax your entire body. When you feel ready, open your eyes and look around you.

What do you see? Look around at all the different colors. Now, you will pull particular colors from the natural scenery surrounding you and bring them inside of yourself with your breath.

First, look for the color red, which will activate chakras one, two, and three. The Sedona rock, from which earth energy spirals out, and the red color of the dirt are optimal for awakening your chakras. Through the perineum, your first chakra, imagine red earth energy coming into your body. This energy comes up to your lower abdomen, your second chakra. Breathe deeply into your lower abdomen, drawing the color red into your lower abdomen. Remembering the red color of the earth, close your eyes and breathe while you imagine the first and second chakras shining brightly with the color red. As the first and second chakras become activated, you will reach optimal vitality and vigor.

Now bring your focus to your solar plexus, the third chakra. Imagine red energy from your lower abdomen rising up to your third chakra. Breathe through your third chakra, inhaling life energy from the air straight into your solar plexus. Imagine your third chakra filling with energy like a balloon filling with air. Now, with your eyes closed, concentrate on your third chakra and imagine your solar plexus glowing with orange light. Will and confidence will surge when your third chakra is activated.

Next, look for the color green, which can help heal your fourth and fifth chakras. As you breathe, draw the green color of the juniper and pine trees into your heart, the fourth chakra. The green energy fills your chest abundantly as you breathe and your chest expands. As you breathe out, the heavy, negative energy in your chest is expelled out of your body. When inhaling, breathe in with your nose and fill your chest with air; when exhaling, breathe out deeply while saying, "hoo." Through your breath, you can expel all negative or stagnant energy from your chest. When your chest feels refreshed, exhale comfortably through your nose. Now close your eyes and imagine the green energy of the trees as you continue to breathe. Pure love radiates from your heart.

Now bring your awareness to your throat, the location of the fifth chakra. Your thyroid glands, which play a role in your emotions, are located here. Among other functions, they control and purify emotional energy so that intense emotions are prevented from going into your brain. When the fifth chakra is weak, it becomes difficult to moderate your emotions, and the emotional energy gives stress to your thyroid glands. As you breathe, draw in the green color of the trees into your throat to heal your fifth chakra. With your eyes closed, picture the color green and imagine that your inner throat shines with a bright green light.

The sixth and seventh chakras may be healed with the blue light of the sky. First, draw the sky's blue light into your third eye, which is located between your eyebrows. Imagine that the blue light penetrates your third eye and continuously flows into the center of your brain, which is also the center of your sixth chakra. As the sixth chakra awakens, a gentle smile emerges on your face. Now close your eyes and remember the blue light of the sky. Imagine the blue light in front of you entering your third eye and filling your entire brain. When your sixth chakra becomes activated, you achieve spiritual awakening, your insight and intuition are increased, and divine energy is awakened.

When your sixth chakra is activated, it naturally influences the seventh chakra. With your eyes closed, imagine that the blue light coming in through the third eye activates your brain and goes straight through the seventh chakra at the crown of your head. Now, imagine that the blue light energy from above the crown of your head spirals down into your brain. You may feel as though there is a weight on the crown of your head, or you may feel like a hole has been opened. Imagine that the light entering your seventh chakra connects down to your first chakra in a straight line. You will feel a sense of complete harmony and integration.

This next Chakra Meditation utilizes the light of the Sedona sunset.

Around the time of sunset, the golden light of the changing sky contains a remarkable healing energy. A magical time of golden light happens only for a brief time during the evening, and this is the best time to awaken the fourth chakra in the heart and the sixth chakra in the brain. Arrive a half hour before the sun sets and loosen your body with some stretches beforehand. Either sit in a half-lotus posture or stand with your feet shoulder width apart.

As the sun starts to sink into the horizon, the golden rays of the sun meet your eyes directly. Extend your arms out so

that the palms of your hands face the sunset. Imagine that the energy of the golden light is coming into your palms and penetrating all the way to your heart chakra in your chest. Golden light energy fills your chest, healing your heart, and the pure energy of love awakens within you. You may move your hands very slowly as they dance in the golden light. Slowly stop moving and sit in a meditation posture. Keep your eyes closed if the glare is too bright. Receive the golden light through your third eye, in between your eyebrows. Your sixth and seventh chakras will awaken as the energy of the golden light fills your brain. Imagine that the golden light passes through the crown of your head down to your perineum and envelops your whole body.

COMMUNICATING WITH TREES

Both Fay Canyon and Boynton Canyon contain old, over-grown trees, which makes them ideal places for practicing communication with trees.

As you walk into the canyon, choose a tree for which you feel an affinity. Avoid trees that are too small and look for a larger-sized tree. There will be a tree feels close to your heart. When you have chosen your tree, get closer so that you are about an arm's length from its leaves.

First, introduce yourself to the tree. You can either do so in your mind or out loud if others are not around you. Tell the tree about your first impression of it. For example, you might say, "Your branches swaying in the wind seemed to be waving hello to me," or "Your sturdy trunk made me feel like I could rely on you, and it made me feel good." Express your heart, however it feels, whatever it may be. You will eventually feel a certain bond with the tree.

Now slowly lift your hands and feel the energy of the tree's leaves. Allow a bit of space between your hands and the leaves, and feel the energy of the leaves with your hands without touching them. Move your hands as if you were caressing the leaves and send the energy coming out from your hands to the tree. The energy of the tree's green color enters your hands, travels up your arms to your shoulders, and spreads throughout your whole body.

Face your palms together and bring them in front of your chest. Feel the energy between your hands through this energy-sensitizing exercise. Spread your hands wide apart as you breathe in and, as you breathe out, bring them back together.

Now the tree's energy enters your body with your breath. Slowly breathe in and receive the tree's fresh oxygen and energy into your body. Slowly breathe out and expel the stagnant energy from your body. Continue this breathing, imagining that pure, healthy life energy is being transferred to your body from the tree. The tree's energy comes into your body, opens its blockages, and activates the circulation in your whole body.

WHOLE BODY WALKING

The hiking trails of Boynton Canyon, which are generally flat and surrounded by many tall trees that emit fresh energy, are ideal for walking meditation.

In our busy lives, it is sometimes hard to find a moment to feel the bottom of our feet. Even when people do have the opportunity to walk, their heads are usually so cluttered with thoughts they are not able to pay any attention to their feet. This is why many people no longer feel grounded and have lost interest in the life that the earth cultivates.

First, relax the tension in your body and stand up straight. Stand so that it feels like there is no empty space between your feet and the ground. As you stand like this, focusing on the bottom of your feet, you will eventually feel all of your weight on your feet. You can feel your entire body's weight at the bottom of your feet without any tension in other parts of your body. You will notice the weight of your body being delivered to the ground and the strength of the Earth that supports that weight.

This isn't merely weight or pressure in the physical sense. It is a real, living sense of life energy. You can feel the vivid feeling of existence, of being alive, as you develop a heart of humble gratitude toward the Earth that nurtures your body and supports your life.

The stronger the feeling is at the bottom of your feet, the stronger the sensation at the crown of your head will be as well. Below you, the land supports you sturdily. Above you, the vast, infinite, empty space is opened for you. Stand with both feet and feel your body, which connects heaven and earth. Below, you can feel your solid legs and lower abdomen filled with abundant energy. Above, you can feel an open heart and a clear, cool head.

Slowly start walking with your senses opened to your body's sensations and to the life energy in the woods. It is important to concentrate on the sensation of the soles of your feet and to not lose awareness of this sensation. The sun's rays, the breeze upon your skin, the smell of the fresh woods, the sound of animals bustling about and birds chirping . . . the sound of your own breath, the sensation of your heartbeat, your skin moist with sweat, the multitude of thoughts running through your head, memories and emotions . . . continue feeling all of these sensations. Do not try to control or hold onto any of these feelings or thoughts, but rather watch them come if they come and go if they go.

When you continue walking like this, your thoughts and emotions will die away, and you will start to feel that you are connected deeply with the woods. When you do Walking Meditation, it is important to pay attention to the woods as a whole—the flowers, trees, wind, and water. You won't be able to feel the surrounding nature properly if you are anxious to take notice of something or if you direct all your attention to only yourself. You will feel the energy that is emitted by the entire woodland if you let go of the urge to fixate your eyes and ears on single objects. You will be able to feel the whole of the forest in its entirety instead of just one flower or tree.

SPIRITUAL BODY MEDITATION

This meditation may be a bit of a challenge for beginners, but it can be a very powerful and precious training for those whose spiritual senses are awakened.

Inside Shaman's Cave, sit comfortably with a straight back and relax your shoulders. Slowly breathe in and breathe out. Lower your hands comfortably onto your knees.

Look over at Secret Mountain in the distance. Relax your eyes and notice where the ridges of Secret Mountain meet the sky. Now close your eyes and imagine you are sitting on top of the ridge you like best. Your spiritual body is sitting right on that ridge. Imagine you are sitting there in a state of pure life energy, as you were before you ever had a body or personality. Your spiritual body is sitting there, emanating such great energy that it covers all of Secret Mountain. You can feel sacredness, nobleness, and fulfillment. Your spiritual body is watching you as you sit in Shaman's Cave.

The strong heartbeat of your spiritual body is emitted into the atmosphere. That heartbeat is delivered to your heart as you sit in Shaman's Cave. Your heart beats more powerfully and vibrantly. The feeling of being alive, the abundant feeling of existence, fills up your entire body. Listen to your heartbeat—one of the strongest life forces in our body—and ask yourself who breathes.

Who am I who sits here?
What is it that I want?

There are times when we become small and narrow-minded, although we know that this is not all that we are. We have countless thoughts, emotions, and habits, but at the same time we also have a mind and eyes that can break free of and watch all of these from a distance. When life becomes hard or lonely, imagine your sacred, undaunted spiritual body sitting on Secret Mountain. Connect your heart with your spiritual body's heart and receive the life force it delivers.

LifeParticles and the MindScreen Meditation

LifeParticles Energy Meditation

Next is a meditation that uses the image of the LifeParticle Sun. Please refer to the image of the LifeParticle Sun on page 157 of this book.

1. Sit comfortably and straighten your neck and your back.

2. Look at the LifeParticle Sun image for one minute. At this time, be careful not to become tense or try too hard to look at the image. As you keep focusing, you may experience the feeling that you're being drawn into the image. You may also feel like the red circle is expanding infinitely around you.

3. Now close your eyes and recreate the LifeParticle Sun in your mind for one minute. (If you want to develop

better concentration, it's also good to keep repeating the process of opening your eyes to look at the image, and then closing them to visualize it in your mind.)

4. With your eyes still closed, imagine the bright light of the LifeParticles coming in through the top of your head and flowing down to your whole body.

5. Breathing comfortably, focus on each part of your body. Imagine the brilliant light flowing down from your head to your forehead, eyes, nose, mouth, tongue, neck, shoulders, arms, and fingertips. Imagine that the light is dissolving any dark, stagnant energy in your body as it flows down. Once again, imagine the light of LifeParticles flowing down from your head to your forehead, eyes, nose, mouth, tongue, neck, chest, abdomen, sides, hips, buttocks, legs, and toes as stagnant energy flows out of your body.

6. Feel your body becoming light as though you've taken a shower with light, and notice sweet saliva pooling in your mouth.

7. Now, with a clear mind, visualize your ideal self, the person you most want to become, for one minute.

8. Travel into the future and see yourself achieving the dreams you wanted to achieve. Imagine yourself celebrating as you overcome the challenges you face. Notice how content and self-assured you are.

9. When you feel satisfied with yourself in your mind, take three deep breaths and slowly open your eyes. Rub your hands and sweep them over your neck and face.

There's no need to feel anxious if you can't see the image of the LifeParticle Sun well when you close your eyes. Your mind's eye may be dark in the early stages. Also, it's possible for you to sense the image even if you can't see the shape or image in your mind. However, if you keep practicing, you will eventually be able to see it vividly in three-dimensional form. The important thing is for you to trust your brain and keep practicing.

MINDSCREEN VISION MEDITATION

This is a vision meditation that utilizes the MindScreen. Practice this meditation for five to ten minutes a day in the morning or evening. Make it your daily routine and ritual. This will help you tremendously in the process of personal re-creation.

Step 1: Establishing a Goal

1. Decide what you want.

2. Check whether that goal is beneficial to others as well as to you, or at least that it is not harmful to anyone. As far as possible, make sure that your desires are compatible with everyone's greatest good.

3. Put your goal in the form of an affirmation. The affirmation must be concise, clear, and positive. Use a present tense, declarative sentence. Here are some examples: "I love doing my work, and I am richly awarded creatively and financially;" "I am living a healthy and abundant life;" "My relationship with my husband is growing happier and more fulfilling every day."

Step 2: Creating an Optimal Energy State

1. Gently shake your head to the left and right, releasing any tension from your neck, and tap your lower

abdomen with loose fists to gather your focus to your lower abdomen.

2. This helps you create the ideal energy state (Water Up, Fire Down) for MindScreen operation. Through these movements, you can feel your head growing cooler and your lower abdomen growing warmer. Your heart and mind will feel peaceful and balanced. This state allows you to create a clear, stable MindScreen without any distorting signals.

Step 3: Connecting with the Flow of LifeParticles

1. Sit in a half-lotus posture or in any comfortable position. Straighten your lower back. Focus on your third eye, which is located between your eyebrows. Imagine bright LifeParticles entering your third eye. Visualize LifeParticles pouring down into your brain and flowing down to your neck, chest, and lower abdomen.

2. Raise your hands and hold them in front of your chest. Bring your palms close together, as if you were praying, but do not let them touch each other. Allowing space between the palms will help maintain the feeling of energy in your hands.

3. Very slowly, move your hands apart from each other and focus on the sensation in the palms. When you have moved them a few inches farther apart, slowly begin to bring them back to the original position again. As

you continue to move your hands closer and farther apart, feel the energy field that exists between them. Focus on the sensation between the palms, imagining that your hands are linked together with energy. As the sensation of energy increases, you will feel a powerful flow of energy not only between your hands but also throughout your whole body.

4. Remember that the whole universe—your body, mind, soul, and all of nature—is made up of the same stuff, the energy you are feeling with your hands now. Remember that right now, in the moment you feel the energy, you are connected with the whole universe.

5. Put your hands down on your knees or make a prayer posture. In that posture, recite your prayer or affirmation. You don't have to speak out loud. Allow your heart to resonate with your affirmation, having deep faith that the affirmation is recognized and accepted.

Step 4: Visualizing Your Goal through Energy

1. Draw what you want on your MindScreen as you continue to feel LifeParticles. Remember that right now, in this moment, you're broadcasting your wish to the whole universe.

2. Your MindScreen is a 360-degree, three-dimensional image. Use your screen to view all of the space around you—above, below, and to your left and right. As you

move your hands freely, make your image concrete by using information from your five senses. Imagine that you are drawing on your MindScreen using the sense of energy you feel in your hands. (Imagine yourself using a big iPad, using your hands to open, close, change the position of, and manipulate various applications. Use all of the space around you as you do this.)

3. Don't simply see your goal. Try to feel it with your sense of touch, listen to it with your sense of hearing, and even detect its taste and smell. Try to hear the voices of people congratulating you on making your wish come true, and even feel the vibration of their hands clapping. The more concrete the image you draw on your MindScreen, the more powerful your prayer becomes.

Step 5: Closing with Deep Gratitude and Joy

1. Slowly bring your hands together in front of your chest. Thank the higher power that permitted all of this with whatever name you choose to use—God, Universe, Higher Self, Cosmic Intelligence, etc. Feel a great sense of joy and gratitude because the process of what you want to become a reality has already started; from a cosmic perspective, it has already been realized.

2. Slowly lower your hands, place them in your lap, and gather your consciousness to your abdomen. End your meditation or prayer with deep breathing.

LifeParticles can transcend time and space. We can send LifeParticles to other people as well as receive them. You may send LifeParticles to people who you love, to family who are far away, or to friends who are unwell. To do so, calm your mind and, with a pure, sincere heart, bring the person to your mind. The moment that you gather your mind and focus on that person, LifeParticles are instantaneously delivered to them.

There are several ways to send LifeParticles. You can deliver them while sitting with a serene mind, or you can do the same while standing. You may want to call the other person beforehand and let them know that you'll be sending LifeParticles to them. Ideally, they should meditate comfortably. You can also ask what parts of their body in particular are bothering them and send LifeParticles to those parts.

For example, you could set a particular time to send LifeParticles to your daughter who lives in a city far away and ask her to meditate at that time. Or you could send LifeParticles while you're meditating quietly so they don't notice. Also, you can use your MindScreen and send LifeParticles to several people at once. If there are a lot of people who come to mind, try the MindScreen Meditation method described below.

1. Sit comfortably and straighten your spine and lower back. Place your hands on your knees with the palms

upward. Close your eyes and focus on your breathing. Take deep breaths regularly, slowly, and naturally.

2. When your mind becomes quiet, imagine that there is a massive screen all around you. This screen is the MindScreen, a screen of light and infinite creation.

3. Call by name, one by one, each person you want to invite to appear on your MindScreen. With your mind's eye, visualize the face of each person you call.

4. When you focus on your mind, you can feel which parts of their body are not healthy, what kind of difficulties they may currently be facing, or what problems they have to solve.

5. Now, you can do it quietly in your mind, or you can extend your hands in front of you and send LifeParticles of love to the people that you invited to your MindScreen.

6. Feel the energy of the people who received LifeParticles becoming brighter and brighter.

7. At this time, something you have wanted to say to someone may suddenly come to mind, or ideas or inspiration for solving a problem may come up.

8. Jot down thoughts and ideas that come up during the meditation in a notebook, and implement them immediately.

9. Write down the people you've sent LifeParticles to and the people you want to send them to in the future in your notebook, and every time you think of them, send LifeParticles of love.

The MindScreen is a transmitting and receiving device for sharing LifeParticles. Like a magnifying glass that gathers light, you can send the powerful energy of LifeParticles through the MindScreen. However, the MindScreen and LifeParticles *must* only be used with a loving heart. Keep in mind that if you imagine a catastrophe wrought upon another person with a desire to harm them or if you send negative energy, that energy will end up coming back to you.

About Ilchi Lee

Ilchi Lee is a respected educator, mentor, and trailblazer devoted to developing the awakened brain and teaching energy principles. For the past thirty years, Ilchi Lee has dedicated his life to helping people become the authors of their lives by harnessing the creative power of the human brain. In that regard, he developed many mind-body training methods, including Dahn Yoga and Brain Education.

Since his first visit to Sedona fifteen years ago, Lee has shared the messages and spirit he has received from Sedona. Lee serves as the president of the University of Brain Education and the International Brain Education Association. He is also the founder of Sedona Mago Retreat, a place for spiritual awakening and holistic learning, located in the wilderness of Arizona's red rock country. He is the author of thirty-three books, including *Healing Society*, *Healing Chakras*, and *Brain Wave Vibration*. For more information, visit www.ilchi.com.

EXPERIENCING ILCHI LEE'S PHILOSOPHY AND METHODS

SEDONA MEDITATION CENTER

The Sedona Meditation Center is a comprehensive hub for meditation that offers both group and individual sessions. A nonprofit organization that welcomes everyone, the meditation center offers programs based on Ilchi Lee's energy principles. *340 Jordan Road, Sedona, AZ 86336, (928) 282-3600*

SEDONA STORY

Sedona Story is a store that features meditation programs, readings, healings, spiritually inspired art, and gifts, including original art and calligraphy by Ilchi Lee. The store runs www.sedonastory.com, a virtual community in which people share their Sedona experiences. *207 N. State Route 89A, Sedona, AZ 86336, (928) 282-3875*

DAHN YOGA

Founded and then passed down by Ilchi Lee, there are over 1,000 locations worldwide that provide Dahn Yoga and Brain Education programs, including about 120 in the United States. They offer group classes and individual sessions in meditative movement and breathing, as well as personal growth workshops. *To find a location near you, visit www.dahnyoga.com or call 877-477-YOGA.*